Spandex Simplified

Sewing for Gymnasts

Happy Sewing!

Marie Porter

Photography by
Michael Porter

Celebration Generation

www.celebrationgeneration.com

Spandex Simplified: Sewing for Gymnasts

First Edition, May 2013

I.S.B.N. 978-0-9850036-3-0

Published and Distributed by

Celebration Generation LLC
P.O. Box 11592
Minneapolis, MN USA
55411

www.celebrationgeneration.com

Cover illustration by Jerry "Jerantino" Minor

Acknowledgments

Another sewing manual, another acknowledgments page to write! The funny thing with these books is that so much of the content was written a long time ago, and all around the same time - the people to thank don't really change from book to book!

As always, I need to thank my grandmother and my late grandfather. They raised me for most of my childhood, and encouraged me to pursue my talents, wherever that would take me. I guess it panned out well - my interests at the time were sewing and cooking!

I couldn't have been all that easy to live with - creativity, a high IQ, Aspergers, and Irish-Canadian stubbornness is a hell of a combination in a kid. Still, they made all kinds of sacrifices to raise me. They kept me entertained ... in figure skating. I'm not sure I could have fallen in love with a more ridiculous sport for two fixed income retirees to finance if I had TRIED.

Despite all of the challenges, they raised me right. I lost my grandfather in the late 90s, but my grandmother has remained the calm - and sane! - in my family's storms ever since. Gramma, your kindness, generosity, and patience were not lost on me. Thank you for everything.

Thank you to my former coach, Gordon Linney... for putting up with me. I was not the most disciplined figure skater ever, he always had to chase me around when I'd skip out on patch, dance, and stroking. To this day, though, I maintain that having a Walkman blasting dance music into my ears was a perfectly acceptable practice tool for surviving patch sessions. Yep, that man had the patience of a saint...

I'd like to thank all of the parents of my fellow skaters that had faith in my sewing and design skills, even at that early age. Your encouragement - and let's be honest, your repeat purchases! - inspired me to stay with it and evolve my skills. As an adult NOW, I have a hard time imagining doing business with a 12 year old... so I now have an even greater appreciation for you all!

Of course, I have to thank my husband. Porter is new to the spandex thing - I didn't meet him til after I had moved on to a new career. With only a vague idea of my past career, he's been incredibly supportive of my spontaneous idea to overhaul my old sewing manuals for re-release. As someone who's been in the same career for a decade and a half at this point, it's got to be weird to deal with my career ADD - but he's getting used to it.

Porter, you're the most sweet, stubborn, romantic, bull-headed, awesome, frustrating, cute, smart, talented, nerdy, handy, and fun man I've ever known. I love you! :)

Table of Contents

Foreword

Having developed a fairly ridiculous career in food / cake / cookbooks, it's kind of easy to forget that I had a whole *other* career before this. I started sewing when I was about 4. My mother bought me one of those toy sewing machines that would "sew" little pieces of foam together. Being the impatient bugger that I am, I soon got tired of it and commandeered my mother's much faster machine - mostly to make Barbie clothes.

When I was 9 or so I took up figure skating. My family was poor, and could not afford the expensive outfits that I would need. I ended up teaching myself how to make these outfits, and soon had a huge, wild wardrobe of skating clothes.. any excuse I could find, I'd make a new one that was "louder" than the last! Eventually, people around the rink started asking me to make them some outfits, they'd wear my stuff to other rinks, and competitions, and word got around. I took my first paying order for a skating outfit at age 11, and have been self employed ever since. Beyond figure skating dresses, I quickly progressed into various other genres of spandex costuming, designing and sewing for dancers, gymnasts, synchro swimmers, pro wrestlers, and more.

After the release of my earlier manual - "Sewing for Skaters and Gymnasts and Dancers ... Oh My!" - I toured Canada and the northern US states, teaching seminars on sewing with spandex. Oh, I had some crazy adventures! I'll never forget the time that my engine blew up on the way home from Minot, ND - I ended up stuck in Steel, ND overnight. It was Kafka-esque, in general... but the highlight was meeting a BIG guy with half his face tattooed blue. It turned out he was an Ultimate Fighter of some sort... as well as a pastry chef who loved Shakespeare. Awesome!

As has been my pattern since I was a kid, I soon succumbed to a combination of boredom and burnout. I'll basically take something up on a lark, be interested... play around with it a bit, get really good at it, and then... I guess it just all becomes routine. When it feels like I've been doing the same thing for just a bit too long, I have to just dump it all and move on to something more entertaining. So, I did.

I was 25. I was also so fried from all of the long hours trying to just keep up with orders, I wanted absolutely nothing to do with spandex ever again. I stopped taking orders, and I discontinued the sewing manuals that I'd written along the way. I took up event floral design, and eventually cake design... and on to cookbooks.

Now, I've come full circle. I felt like I had all of this knowledge sitting in the back of my head - and in forgotten folders on my computer - just gathering virtual dust and cobwebs. I decided that it was time to revisit them. This book is an elaboration on the concepts and techniques in my original manual, edited specifically for gymnasts, updated with photos, diagrams, and new styles. All of the information provided is still current and applicable.

I've always believed that home made is the best way to go when it comes to spandex costuming- saves a lot of money, and lets you be creative.. you can really do whatever you want! I hope that you not only learn a lot from this book, but also have a lot of fun with it. With just a few basic skills, spandex can be SO much fun to work with! I hope you're able to get the same sort of joy from working with it, that I experienced all of those years ago!

- Marie

Basic Principles of Leotard Design

Proper Fit and Design Considerations

Beyond almost anything else - colour, style, etc - a leotard should fit well, and this means that it will not cut in at the legs, arms, neck, or anywhere else.

Once you make your first leotard from a given pattern, try it on the intended wearer and have her move around. It should lie flat against the skin, and not bunch or pucker much when she moves. A leotard that wrinkles on the sides when you move is too long in the body.

Another thing to take into account is the specific needs of the wearer. Is this a person who becomes overheated while training, and would benefit from a sleeveless garment with cut out back, or is this person going to prefer full coverage? How much are they intending to abuse this garment? If the gymnast tends to ruin leotards easily, try to keep it as simple as possible, using durable fabrics and embellishment techniques, if so desired.

Each style of gymnastics comes with its own set of rules regarding clothing, and that is something that should be kept in mind when designing competition leotards. As an example, I believe that most branches of gymnastics require that leotard necklines be cut no lower than the shoulder blades, and that leg openings cannot be any higher than hip height. (Except rhythmic, which specifies nothing over waist height!)

"Gymnastics" encompasses so many different disciplines - artistic, rhythmic, trampoline, tumbling, acrobatic, aerobic... it's always best to consult the rules of your particular sport when it comes to competition attire.

Figure Flaw Camouflage

Does your gymnast have any potential figure flaws that you want to cover up, or aspects that you would like to play up? A very general rule of thumb is that if there is a problem area of the figure, accentuate a different area to distract the eye. For instance, if you are self conscious of your waist/hip area, then make the lower part of the garment in a solid colour like black, and have the upper part be a bright colour, or bold print. Have a funky neckline, interesting sleeve, or an interesting trim near the top, to distract the eye.

A few general guidelines:

Legs: Legs can be made to look longer and leaner by cutting the leg openings a bit higher. Placing the skirt (when applicable) a little bit higher that normal on the sides, without adding compensation length to the skirt will also make the torso look shorter, lengthening the appearance of the legs.

Waist:	Distract the eye as described above. Use colour blocking to accentuate the waist, or to give the illusion of a narrow waist on a blocky figure - have hourglass shaped colour blocking down the front of the leotard to trick the eye into seeing a narrower waist.
Long Torso:	A woman's torso can appear long if her legs are disproportionally short. Horizontal lines can shorten the appearance of the torso. Again, skirt placement can help, when applicable.
Butt:	Distract the eye, as described above. Higher cuts for the leg openings also help.
Short Torso:	If you have a short torso, you will want to draw the eye up, away from the waist. Vertical or diagonal stripes (or design elements) can help to lengthen the torso, and you can experiment with colour blocking to aid you in this.
Larger Legs:	If the legs are larger due to being well muscled, or you aren't too worried about them, showing more leg with a high cut bottom works well. Low cut bottoms aren't a good idea when combined with larger legs, as they may create unwanted lumps in the leotard.

Just as you can use distraction to draw the eye away from problems, you can also use it to draw attention TO areas in other ways.

- If your body is rather boxy, you can use a vivid waistband accent to give the illusion of a waist.

- If you want to appear less flat chested, you can give the appearance of a bustline by using advancing colours (bright) around the chest, especially combined with an interesting neckline.

- Are really proud of your sculpted shoulders? The arm openings should angle in towards the neck a bit, instead of straight up.

As far as distracting and attracting colours go, this is basically the scoop: advancing colours are the ones that stand out, and grab the eye first - bright, bold, or light colours, big prints. Receding colours are the ones that fall into the background when contrasted with a bright colour. These are darker colours, like black and navy blue. These are the colours you should use when you want the eye to go elsewhere.

All of these ideas can be combined for an overall flattering leotard. Remember these guidelines, and experiment with the design of your leotard:

- Vertical lines add length, and slenderize the torso. Horizontal lines shorten and broaden the torso. Beware though, WIDE stripes can have the opposite effect! (A torso divided into 3 wide, horizontal line may look longer than it actually it.)

- Diagonal lines can slenderize, and will sometimes add or reduce torso length, depending on the angle. The closer to horizontal the lines are, the more that the rules for horizontal will apply. The closer to vertical (steeper angle) the lines are, the vertical rules are more likely to apply. Once again, really wide stripes can provide an effect opposite to the main rule.

- Curved lines soften the figure, and will make it appear to be more curvy. This can be achieved through colour blocking, cut, or both.

- Dark or matte fabrics can make the body look smaller, as they absorb light

- Shiny or bright fabrics can make a very thin body look a bit larger, as they reflect light. This makes the shiny fabric "advancing", regardless of the colour. While black is a receding colour, very shiny black becomes advancing. In this case, you'd want to use matte black to hide, shiny black to draw the gaze / accentuate.

- Light colours visually add pounds to a body

- Square necklines can disguise smaller bust lines, but also give coverage to a larger bust

Designing for the Gymnast

Discuss your ideas with the wearer. Ask for any opinions, and what aspects they like about their current and previous garments. Do not be afraid to try something new, but also be sure to work within their comfort zones if necessary. If a gymnast is uncomfortable with what they are wearing, it will likely come out - negatively - in their movements and performance.

Be sure to talk to the coach. Many times, a coach will have a general idea of what they'd like to see done for a competition leotard. Even if they leave it completely up to you, run your design by the coach before going to buy your fabric.

When you are designing competition leotards, there are several factors which go into making a leotard suit the wearer. Even the most beautiful competition leotard can look just plain weird on the wrong person. For instance, a person's look and personality play a strong role in deciding how the finished garment should look. While competition leotards may end up being suited towards a character, role, or theme being portrayed, they should also reflect the personality and attitude of the wearer.

As an example, if the wearer is a sporty, no nonsense athlete, odds are, they won't want something super "girlie". Try to keep the lines simple, basic colours, and no frills. Outgoing people look good in bright colours and bold prints, sharper lines, etc, while quiet people tend to be more suited to muted colours, softer lines, and small prints. When in doubt, ask the gymnast and/or coach for an opinion.

Designing for the Music

What do you think of when you are listening to the music that will be used? What mental imagery comes to mind? A good idea for when you are designing a competition leotard, is to write down words that come to your mind when listening to the music, and elaborate on those ideas. Talk to the coach. Sometimes, they will have a specific design, or even a small concept, of what they would like the garment to look like, or could advise you of where to start.

In the case of soundtrack music from movies or musicals, it is usually a good idea to watch the movie or musical in question. Although you are not bound to borrow your design directly from something you see, it can definitely help to get the creative juices flowing.

What kind of mood is the music? Will people associate it with a particular period, artist, film, etc? Though it is a good idea to not "typecast" your leotard, sometimes a piece of music will be such that a certain theme of leotard is pretty much required, or will almost look out of place. A more modern leotard will not look appropriate with baroque music, and a jazzy, neon, sequined leotard will look out of place with the theme from Robin Hood.

Another good source of ideas is the local library, especially for period music. No judge is really going to care if you wear a leotard with Elizabethan style influences for a Victorian piece of music, but it can't hurt to look into it. Although some aspects of period costumes are impractical to duplicate in a leotard, take a look at some other details. Huge portrait collars may not work, but what about the sleeve? Style of trim? Maybe a design element or motif that can be done in applique...

Listen to the music, close your eyes, and see what comes to mind... a colour, shapes, style, or whatever. It's a good way to start.

Visibility

Designing for visibility is incredibly important! One thing that I cannot stress enough: What looks good up close won't necessarily look good, or even show up that well from across the gym/arena. Conversely, what doesn't look all that great up close may look amazing from a distance. A few considerations:

Distance: You know how you're supposed to exaggerate the makeup for competition? You'd never send your gymnast to school looking like that! It's because from a distance, small details do not show up as well, and you NEED to exaggerate. The makeup principle also applies to decoration of a garment. Don't drive yourself crazy spending months beading an leotard that is meticulous. Odds are, it will show up as just a general sparkle. Individual seed beads DO NOT show up on the floor, so don't even bother. If you want a rounded bead effect, go for the chuckier Rocaille beads. There's no real need for meticulous accuracy. Also, small variations in colour will not show up, it will all look as if it is one colour.

Effect: Beads and sequins are primarily used for sparkle, not colour. Using a few colours of sequins won't necessarily show up. In order to get the best sparkle for your effort, make sure to use faceted sequins, not the flat ones. When selecting beads to use, try to get the kind with the metallic silver coloured lining, preferably square cut (faceted) on the inside. This allows for the best reflection of light, ie. sparkle. Unlined beads don't have much sparkle to them at all.

Lighting: Fabrics look much different under the fluorescent lights used in most gyms/arenas, so taking a sample piece of fabric to the venue is usually a good idea, to see how it looks.

Intended Use: Is this leotard ONLY going to be used in performance, or are you making it for an accomplished competitor who will probably need it for publicity photographs and award photos, etc? If it's only being used in competition, it doesn't really matter how accurate your beading is, but if it will be used in close-up photos, you may want to be a little more meticulous about it.

Functionality

First and foremost, leotards are *sportswear*. They are active wear, and are pretty useless if they hamper the gymnast's range of motion or confidence. Use good, durable fabric with a good amount of stretch. Take care of the leotard, rinsing well with every use. Hand wash competition leotards, and always air dry - Never in the washing machine, never put them in the dryer. Taking care of the base fabric of your leotard will make it last!

Zippers can be a touchy issue. Personally, I have no use for them. The thing with zippers is that they were not intended to be used on stretch fabrics in the first place, and every time you add something like a zipper into a seam, that is introducing a point of weakness to the garment. As a bit of trivia, many professional ballet dancers (I've been told Russian ballet dancers in particular) don't even use zippers in their costumes, they are sewn in to them.

I'd be willing to bet that most, if not all "performance athletes" (Figure skaters, gymnasts, synchro skaters, etc) have either busted a zipper, seen someone bust a zipper, or heard a story about someone busting a zipper in competition. Aside from the fact that a zipper busting is very embarrassing and a hassle, even just having a zipper can add worry to an athlete's mind during the competition. As stress can negatively impact performance, I find it best to just steer clear of zippers. "I hope my zipper doesn't break", as a stress, can be avoided by not having one to worry about - leaves more time to worry about sticking that landing!

When designing a leotard, another major consideration to take into account is the gymnasts' safety, as well as the safety of other gymnasts. First and foremost, ensure that all leotards are well fitted. Leotards that are baggy run the risk of getting caught on apparatus. Any attachments, such as sequins, rhinestones, and beads, should be SECURELY attached. No one wants to land barefoot on a jagged piece of rhinestone or sequin!

Colour Theory

Colour is one of your first considerations, as it will affect your choice of fabric. Using the gymnasts' favourite colour isn't necessarily the best idea, sometimes it will not suit their skin colouring. A few rules to take into consideration.

Skin Tone: A pale skinned person will look washed out in a really dark colour, and will look ghostly in a light colour. Try to keep it at a happy medium. Medium to darker skinned people have a greater choice in what they can wear. Always hold a fabric up to your face to see how it looks against your skin. Another consideration for would be acne. Does your gymnast have acne or facial blemishes? If so, a red or pink leotard would not be a good idea, as it would only spotlight the blemishes and make them more pronounced.

Hair Colour: Some hair colours just look better with certain colours than others. A great example of this would be red haired people wearing green. Make sure that the garment colour works with the hair colour. Of course, this is coming from someone with a penchant for dyeing her hair bright turquoise...

Personality: An outgoing person usually looks good in colours that are vibrant, while shy and quiet types usually look better in lighter colours. This can also be a comfort issue, as some people just don't feel comfortable wearing loud colours.

To get a general idea of colour personalities, here's a rough guide. Keep in mind that this is not an exact science, but many times, people are surprised at the accuracy. This is paraphrased from something from way back in fashion design school:

Red: Red tends to represent positive, aggressive, passionate people.

Orange: Orange tends to represent social, outgoing people.

Yellow: Yellow tends to represent complicated people. Abstract thinkers, intelligent, and often idealistic.

Green: Green tends to represent well balanced, realistic people.

Blue: Blue tends to represent cautious, wise, level headed people

Purple: Purple tends to represent passion, mourning, regal people

In addition to actual colour, colour types / vibrance levels also have personality profiles associated with them. This is the saturation or brightness of the actual colours.

Bright: Uncomplicated, "What you see is what you get", direct personality.

Pastels: Shyness, introversion

Intense: Creativity and independence.

Mid tones: Any extremes in colour personality are tempered by judgement, conservatism.

Subdued: Sophistication and wisdom

Colour Terminology

It might be nice if you knew all the different terms you're going to hear when it comes to colour, huh? A basic rundown of it goes like this:

Hue :   This is a colour's name, what you know it by. Pink, Blue, Red, Yellow, are all Hues.

Value: This talks about the colours appearance - brightness, darkness, or how bright / bold it is.

Tint: The colour produced when you mix a Hue with White. Pink is a Tint of Red.

Shade: The colour produced when you mix a Hue with Black.

Tone: The colour produced when you mix a Hue with Grey. This is done to lessen a colour's intensity. Think "Toning Down" the colour.

Primary: Red, Yellow, and Blue

Secondary: Orange, Green, and Violet

Tertiary: Red-Orange, Yellow-Orange, Yellow-Green, Blue-Green, Blue-Violet, Red-Violet

Colour Schemes

When using more than one colour, either in colour blocking, appliques, or accessories, you might want to look into using an organized scheme to choose which colours to use.

Monochromatic: The word Monochromatic comes from two Greek words: *Monos*, meaning single, and *Chroma*, meaning colour. This colour scheme involves using tints, tones, and shades of any ONE particular colour , together.

Analogous: An analogous colour scheme involves using colours that are so close to each other on the colour wheel, they don't create a sharp contrast. For example: Red, Red-Orange, and Orange, used together, would be an analogous colour scheme. This allows for a little diversity with use of colour, while still remaining conservative.

Complimentary: Using two colours that are directly opposite each other on the colour wheel. Examples would include Blue & Orange, Yellow and Violet, Red & Green, etc

Split Complementary: For a similar effect as the complimentary colour scheme, that is more mild on the eyes, you could try a split complementary colour scheme. For this, you would choose one main colour, for example, Blue. Instead of using the complimentary colour to your main one (orange), you would use the tertiary colours on either side of the compliment (Red-Orange and Yellow-Orange).

Triad: To create a triadic colour scheme, you would choose 3 colours, shades, tints, or tones that are at equidistant points on your colour scheme. That is to say, if you were to place an equilateral triangle on your colour wheel, the colours at each of the 3 points would be a triadic colour scheme. For example: Red, Yellow, and Blue is triadic, so is Violet, Green, and Orange

Colour Wheel

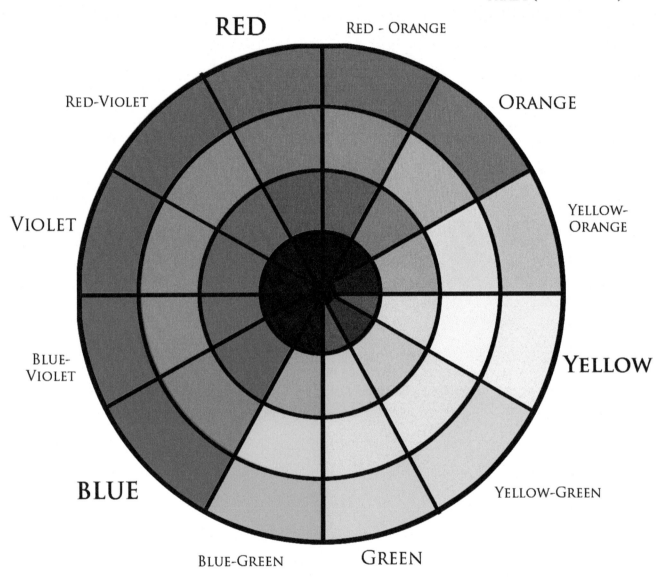

RED

RED - ORANGE

RED-VIOLET

ORANGE

VIOLET

YELLOW-ORANGE

BLUE-VIOLET

YELLOW

BLUE

YELLOW-GREEN

BLUE-GREEN

GREEN

PRIMARY COLOURS
SECONDARY COLOURS
TERTIARY COLOURS

Unity

What is design unity? This is actually a hard thing for me to describe, but easy to pick out in a finished garment. Unity is how all of the elements of your leotard work together to make a pleasing, and visually balanced finished garment.

You don't want to overdo your design, making it too "busy" to look at. Don't try to throw in all kinds of design elements at once. For example:

If you have a really interesting fabric, say a metallic hologram, be careful with beading / sequinning it, and don't go overboard with the actual cut of the leotard - all kinds of funky design elements, cut aways, etc. Let the fabric speak for itself

In short, have one main "interest" element of your leotard, and concentrate on that. Main elements would be things like fabric, colour, texture, shape of the design, and embellishments. (Rhythmic leotards tend to bend the unity rules, going for far more flamboyant and "busy" designs!)

Another form of unity to consider - which is definitely open to interpretation - is how a colour or fabric can be used pleasingly. For example, pale colours look best in "feminine" designs - curved lines, soft textures etc. Anything with harsh, geometric lines may look slightly out of place.

In the situation of funky fabrics, such as hologram... less is better. If you use one of these fabrics in a full coverage leotard for a team, there is a good chance that it will look like "too much". Take it easy, and use these fabrics sparingly. The fabric can be used successfully, as long as you have, say, an open back, and lower neckline. If in doubt, ask someone. A trusted opinion can mean the difference between an amazing leotard, and fashion disaster.

Selecting Fabrics

For basic (practice) leotards, basic Nylon-spandex is the most popular, affordable, and versatile choice. Spandex can be either 2 way stretch, meaning it will stretch along EITHER the length OR width, or 4 way stretch, meaning it will stretch along BOTH the length AND the width.

4 way stretch, generally speaking, is a higher quality than 2 way stretch and is much more desirable to use in your projects. 4 way provides a much more comfortable fit, is less prone to ripped seams, and is definitely worth paying the extra money for. 2 way stretch fabric sometimes has a tendency to fray or pull, and is sometimes more sheer than the 4 way stretch. 4 way stretch fabric makes a more durable, comfortable garment basc. I wouldn't recommend using 2 way stretch fabrics for anything but applique designs.

When using a print, check to see if there is a linear design to it, whether that be stripes, banding, gradient, or whatever. If there is, be sure that you will like the way the design looks with the greatest degree of stretch going across the body. Don't cheat and make your leotard with the stretch going up and down, or it won't fit right, and could be quite uncomfortable even if it does end up "fitting".

Another thing to keep in mind about purchasing fabric is the actual quality of the fabric. If you pull on an edge, and see little white elastic fibres, it's a cheap fabric, and isn't very durable. Also, see if it goes see-through when you stretch it. Fabric like this has a tendency to wear down a lot faster than not. Spend the few extra dollars buying decent fabric up front, instead of spending more time and money a few months down the line to re-do it.

Basic nylon spandex comes in varying qualities, prices, colours, weights and textures. It can be plain, printed, or even embellished with a bit of glitter accent, as in the blue fabric swatch above. Aside from basic nylon spandex, there are a few other choices:

"Moleskin" Spandex:

This is a heavy 4-way stretch spandex. It looks basically the same as normal spandex, with a few differences. Moleskin Spandex is heavier, and comes in limited colours. .

Cotton Spandex:

As with nylon Spandex, cotton Spandex comes in varying colours, qualities, and weights. Cotton Spandex is most suitable for shorts, sports bras, and garments of that nature - not as much for leotards.

Power Mesh:

Power mesh is sometimes used like illusion for the body of garments, but usually, it is used on the inside of garments as a "girdle" effect. Tummy panels are usually made of power mesh. It can be 2 way or 4 way stretch, and is quite durable. Power mesh comes in black, white, and flesh tone.

Swimsuit Lining

Swimsuit lining is usually not visible when the suit is being worn - Aside from through sheer sections - but is an important part of your fabric selection, when applicable. (Gymnasts tend to buy separate liner garments, rather than line their leotards). Generally speaking, it will be beige coloured. As with most fabrics discussed here, there is good swimwear lining... and then, there is NOT good lining. Distinguishing between the two can be tricky, especially when dealing solely with text! Good swimwear lining feels durable and substantial, with a good amount of 4 way stretch. When stretched, it will not "run". Low quality swimwear lining feels more flimsy, and tends to only have 2 way stretch to it.

Illusion (AKA "Glistenette") and Stretch mesh:

Illusion and stretch mesh are sheer fabrics which are available in many colours (including flesh-tone), and as either a 2 way or 4 way stretch. Illusion tends to have a tight, "solid" appearance, with a shimmery look to the right side - though either side can be used. Stretch mesh has a matte finish, with a more open... well, MESH appearance . Either can be used for cutouts, or to resemble skin - though Illusion's shimmer doesn't make for very realistic "skin". Mesh is used extensively for rhythmic leotards.

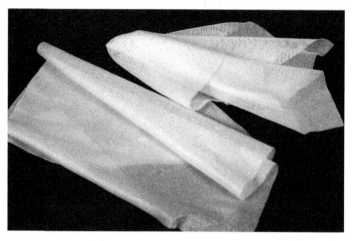

In this photo, an example of Illusion / Glistenette can be seen to the lower left, with a similar colour of stretch mesh in the upper right. Notice the difference in "weave" / texture. The beige variety of stretch mesh is used frequently in leotards and other stretch costuming. As it has no sparkle to it, it makes a good alternative to illusion for a skin tone effect when a particularly invisible effect is desired. When a darker colour than the standard beige is desired, stretch mesh is easily dyed with tea or coffee.

To custom tint skin-toned stretch mesh, start with beige coloured fabric. Decide how much darker you will need it - for "tan" colours, use tea. For darker brown colours, use coffee. Brew a fairly strong batch of tea or coffee, place the hot liquid into a large pot.. Bring the liquid to a boil, add a small scrap of your stretch mesh fabric, and remove from heat. Allow fabric to steep in the tea for at least 20 minutes before rinsing. If the colour is right, dye the rest of your fabric - I recommend dyeing a LOT of it, and keeping it on hand. If the colour needs to be darker, add more tea or coffee (instant works), and try again.

Tea-Dyed Stretch Mesh - Before and After

Note: Stretch mesh differs from "Power" mesh in that it feels much less "structured", more delicate. Stretch mesh wouldn't work for a girdle effect, and you would not want to use power mesh for the "skin tone" design effect that stretch mesh is usually used for.

Hologram Spandex:

Hologram spandex is a plain spandex with reflective bits of foiling fused onto it into various patterns - star bursts, snake skin print, or geometric tessellations. Hologram Spandex is usually pretty expensive, ranging from $30 - $50 per metre for decent quality, sometimes even more. Although this fabric is very cool, and you may be tempted to make an entire leotard out of it, be forewarned - this stuff can really be a case of "too much of a good thing". Note: when the metallic dots are extremely small and close together, the fabric usually goes by the name "mystique" - and it's quite popular for gymnastics use!

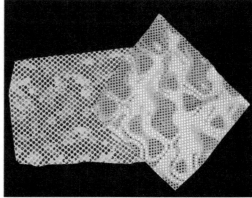

Metallic / Foil Spandex

Metallic Spandex started out mostly in gold and silver, but was soon available in many colours - if you search for it. This is a really high quality spandex with 4 way stretch, great recover ability, and is easy to sew with. The metallic effect is non-holographical, just a smooth, solid effect of metal. I've also seen this fabric referred to as "liquid gold" "liquid metal", and "liquid silver", but that can get confusing with the non-spandex fabric of the same name.

Metallic Spandex can be tricky to buy, as there are many cheap stretch fabrics out there, with the same sort of look. The rule of thumb I've found: if the metallic finish is printed on to a coordinating colour spandex, it's probably the good, 4 way stretch fabric. This is far more durable than the cheaper version, which is usually printed on a very thin, white spandex.

Foil Print Spandex:

This fabric is plain or printed Spandex, with accents of foil embossed on it. (Not a solid foil)

Usually only available through mail order, foil spandex is a little expensive, and doesn't always have the best stretch both ways - it's usually a 2 way stretch fabric. Faults aside, foil print spandex has a very nice effect when light shines on it.

Spandex - Backed / Stretch Velvet:

This is not to be confused with Panne velvet. Stretch Velvet tends to cost much more than Panne, usually around $30-$50 ish per metre, as opposed to around $10 per metre.

Spandex backed velvet should have a 4 way stretch, and can come in either flat / plain, or "crushed" (textured) varieties. Additionally, some varieties have glittery designs embellished right onto them.

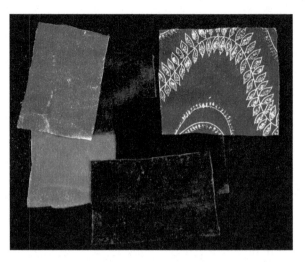

Special care should be taken to make sure all pieces are cut with the fabric "pointing" in the same direction (nap). If you run your hand up and down the fabric (ACROSS the greatest degree of stretch), it will either feel smooth, or rough. If you cut your front pieces so the fabric feels smooth going from top to bottom, be sure to cut your back piece the same way, or it will look like two totally different colours of fabric, on the floor!

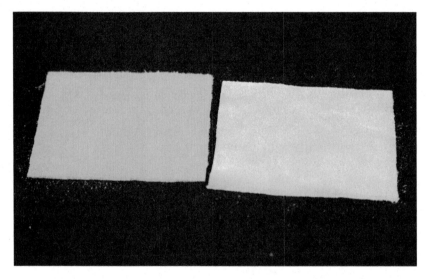

Two pieces of the same fabric, with smoothness facing opposite directions. Big difference!

In contrast to good stretch velvet, panne velvet tends to default as a crushed, textured appearance, and is rather cheap. It is only a 2 way stretch fabric. While it's OK (JUST "ok"!)for accents, skirts, sleeve inserts, etc... I'd suggest just steering clear of it, entirely.

Stretch Chiffon:

Stretch chiffon looks almost like a cross between illusion, and power mesh. Stretch chiffon is a 2 way stretch fabric, and is economically priced. It does not fray or unravel in the same way normal chiffon does. Stretch chiffon is good for thinly layered rhythmic skirts, but doesn't see a whole lot of use in gymnastics leotards.

Basic Pattern Alterations

Measuring

Because spandex stretches, it's fairly easy to get a commercially-bought pattern to fit, as the stretchiness will allow for minor variations in measurements. Before you figure out which size to start with, though, you will need to take some measurements. Accurate measurements go a long way to ensuring a final product that fits! The most common measurements needed include:

Chest / Bust: Measuring across the fullest part of the chest. Usually across the nipple line.

Underchest / Under Bust / Ribcage: Measured under the breasts, where the bra band would go.

Waist: Smallest part of waist. If you have trouble finding it, have the gymnast bend to one side. The point at which the torso bends is the waist line.

Hips: Measure around the widest part, straight across the fullest part of the butt - NOT the actual hip bones up front.

Back-waist: From the prominent vertebra in the neck, down the back to the waistline. (Some patterns require a full torso measurement. As they can differ on how it's taken, it's best to consult the package instructions on the patterns requiring this measurement.)

- The person being measured should not take their own measurements. When one measures themself, they tend to screw up their posture and get inaccurate readings.

- When taking the back-waist measurement, have the gymnast stand with their back to the person taking measurements. They should stand straight, and bend their head down to the front. The bone that sticks out in the base of the neck is referred to as the "prominent vertebra". They should be measured from this bone, down to the back of their waistline. If the person taking measurements is new to doing so, their should put a belt on / tie something around the gymnast's actual waistline, so there's no guessing as to where it actually is.

- Make sure that the measuring tape goes straight around the body, not scooping or dipping anywhere, and that it does not twist when you're doing so. This is especially important when taking the bust measurement, as most people tend to let the measuring tape dip under the shoulder blades on this measurement!

Using a Pattern

I like to use rolls of medical exam table paper for patterns. Basically, open up your "master" pattern - the store bought pattern. Don't ever do anything to that pattern - you can use it for many, many projects, if you trace it each time you need to make a new size/shape leotard! Just line up one long end of exam table paper with the "fold" line of the pattern (the black line below), if applicable. The store bought pattern will be clearly visible through the exam table paper - trace your desired size on to the exam table paper, and there you go!

You'll notice that I don't have skirt lines on the following diagrams. I strongly believe that you should have a well fitting torso / body suit pattern, before deciding on where to cut for the skirt line. Generally speaking, the skirt lines that come with commercially available patterns are not flattering at all, so I recommend ignoring them entirely.

Sizing a Pattern

When choosing which size of pattern to make, compare your measurements to the chart provided on the pattern. If your measurements fit various sizes (for instance, the chest is a "large", waist "small", and hips "medium"), use the pattern guide for the largest size represented, in this case, a large. When transferring your pattern, you will be making a few minor alterations to the (in this case) hip and waist sizes.

While you may be able to use one of the provided sizes without alteration, there's a good chance that you'll want to adjust the sizing. Using the example above - Overall a "Large", but "Small" waist and "Medium" hips - this is how you would trace out your new pattern:

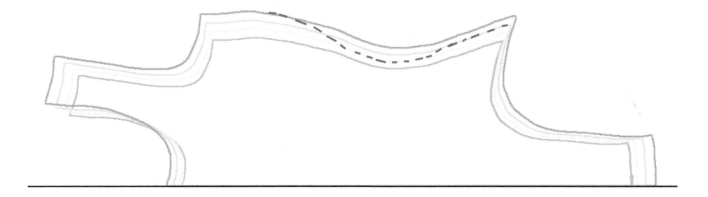

In this example, Pink = XS, Yellow = Small, Green = Medium, Blue = Large

For the top and bottom of the leotard, trace along the blue outline. From the chest down, you'll want to gradually transition from the blue line to the yellow line, right about where the waist is. As you continue downward, transition out to the green line for the hips. Just freehand it, and don't worry - Spandex is very forgiving!

There are several different pattern brands out there. I always liked the Kwik Sew brand, as they were not only easy to use (Printed on actual paper, not tissue!), but they were very true-to-size, and used a center back seam. (A pattern with a curved centre back seam will lie flatter and fit nicer than one that has a straight centre back seam, or one that has the back cut as one piece.) Again... the skirt lines on their patterns aren't the best, and should be ignored - look for a swimsuit or bodysuit pattern, if desired! A list of pattern companies and other references is located at the back of this manual.

Before we get into the specifics of altering a pattern for length or shape, there are a couple basic bits of information that are good to know:

- The majority of teen/adult sized patterns are designed to fit up to a C-cup chest. If your gymnast is larger-busted, altering the bustline will result in a more comfortable garment. Adding extra length and width through the front will help it fit over the longer bust curves, as shown below. For every size above a C cup, add about ½ cm, or .25 inch in length. This should be done at the widest part of the chest (on the pattern), using the technique below for adding length.

- The alterations you make to add or remove length will need to be done at the same points on both the front and back of the pattern - and commercially available patterns will have lines marked for this purpose. Where you make the alteration will depend on the gymnast's body. If the length (or lack thereof) is in the upper torso (if the gymnast is long or short waisted), then make your adjustment above the waist line. If the gymnast is long or short in the lower torso, adjust below the waistline. If the gymnast's body is proportionate, you can adjust both above and below the waist. (That is, if a major adjustment needs to be made, make 2 adjustment sites on either side of the garment, one above, and one below the waist, of equal amounts)

Generally speaking, though, you will likely only find yourself needing to add an inch or so in length - which is fine to do above the waist.

Adding Length

1.   Mark a straight line across your traced pattern, where you want to make the alteration.

2.   Cut the pattern at this line. Have a piece of paper handy.

3.   Tape one half of the pattern to this piece of paper, with the majority of the paper extending past the cut edge, towards where the other piece of the pattern would be.

4.   Find out how much you will be adding (say 1 inch, for demonstrative purposes). On either side of the cut edge of the pattern (centre and side), mark a spot 1 inch away from the pattern edge, and connect the two marks with another straight line.

5.   Take the other pattern piece, and line it up against this new line, so that it also lines up with the first pattern piece. Tape it down. See the diagram on following page.

6.   Draw a new edge to the pattern on the paper, where it would have been if not for the alteration. You may need to curve it slightly to fit a more natural path than just a straight line.

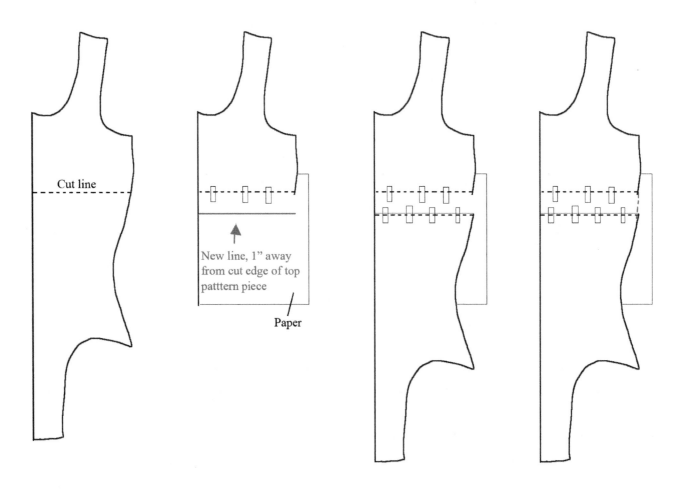

7.   Repeat for the other side of the pattern. Ie: this diagram shows a front pattern piece - the same extension would need to be applied to that pattern piece for the back of the leotard.

Removing Length

1.   Mark a line straight across the pattern in the place you would like to make the alteration.

2.   Mark lines on either side of the original line, that are ½ of the amount you would like to remove. (In the case of a 1 inch alteration, you would mark .5 inch above, and .5 inch below the original line.)

3.   Fold the pattern in half along the MIDDLE line.

4.   Fold the pattern again, along one of the other two lines. You should now have the two outside lines touching each other, with a .5 inch fold (Assuming a 1" alteration, as example).

5.   Tape the fold down, keeping the two outer lines touching each other.

6.   Draw new edges in. It may be necessary to trim corners, in order to give it a natural curve.

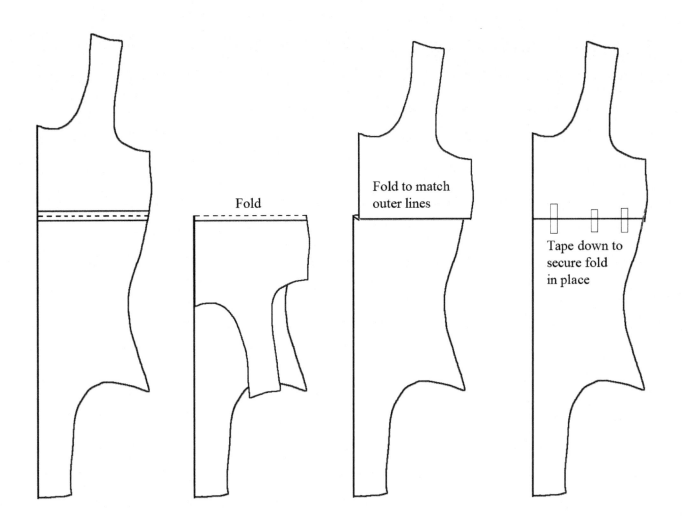

7.   Repeat for the other side of the pattern. Ie: this diagram shows a front pattern piece - the same extension would need to be applied to that pattern piece for the back of the leotard.

Now, these were the methods that I started with, back when I first started costuming. There is a quicker and easier way, in my opinion... and this is how I've done it for years!:

1.   Lay the master pattern out, with piece of tracing paper on top. Line edge of paper up with fold line, if applicable. Trace out the top part of the pattern, as well as the cut line.

2.   Move the tracing paper to separate the traced cut line from the original cut line, by the distance needed to move (eg: 1" separation). Be sure that you are moving the paper directly to one side, so everything still lines up well (even if you'll have to draw in new lines.). To lengthen, move the traced portion away from the portion yet to trace, to shorten, move the traced portion towards the portion left to trace.

3. Continue tracing the remaining portion of the pattern, drawing/smoothing a new connecting edge if necessary.

4. Repeat with the other side of the pattern.

Adjusting Curve of the Back

You may find, once you've made your first leotard, that there seems to be extra fabric in the small of the gymnast's back, that the leotard is not laying flat against her skin. If this is the case, she probably has a deeper curve to her back than the pattern you are using was intended for. Don't worry though, many people do!

To correct this, simply draw a deeper curve to the pattern. Your curve will start at the shoulder blades (widest part of the chest on the pattern), curve in to the smallest part of the waist, and back out to meet up with the widest part of the bum.

Start with taking about an inch off the original pattern (at the waist), and experiment until it fits right.

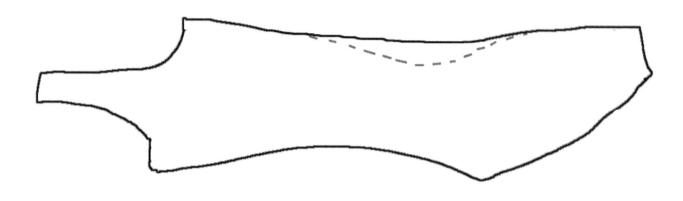

Adjusting the Butt Length

You may find, once you've made your first leotard, that there seems to be extra fabric - vertically - in the butt of the leotard. When this is the case, it can look bunched up towards the bottom of the butt, while fitting fine, side-to-side. While I love Kwik Sew patterns, this was an issue I had to correct almost as a default correction, when it came to "Misses" sizes (ie: XS, S, M, L, XL).

To correct this, figure out how much fabric you have as excess in the back of the . Just pinch it - vertically along the center back seam - until it fits snugly. However much you pinched off is the amount you'll need to remove from the pattern.

It's probably easier to show, THEN explain:

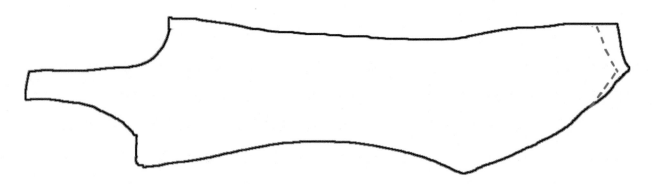

I would make a mark about 2" up the center back seam, measured from the bottom/crotch seam. I would also measure about 1" up the bottom of the leg seam, and draw a curved new cut line between the 2" and 1" marks.

From there, I would measure the length of the bottom seam, and transfer that to the new cut seam - measuring out from the center back seam. Mark that spot, then taper the existing leg curve in to meet the mark on the new cut line.

This simple alteration will make leotards made by a Kwik Sew pattern fit a LOT better. While the measurements given are the default I'd suggest on that particular brand of pattern, the technique can be used to fix a "saggy bum" in any brand of pattern.

Adjusting Leg Openings

While the leg openings on a commercial pattern may be just fine as it is, it is an area where you can provide some customization to fit and flatter, or just for comfort. Deciding where you want the new leg cut line will be partially a matter of preference (Or the gymnast/parent/coach, usually!), and partially a matter of trial and error. (Remember to check with current competition rules regarding acceptable leotard styles!)

After making all of the adjustments that you want for size and length, make a practice leotard - including elastic in all of the openings that need them- leg/arm/neck. Use the practice leotard as a guide to where you want to adjust the leg hole, if at all. While the gymnast is wearing the test leotard, mark the desired leg height with a safety pin.

Have the gymnast change out of the leotard, and examine it. Measure up the side seam, from the edge to the safety pin. This is how much length you will need to remove from the side seam on the pattern, both front and back.

Let' s look at some basic leg alterations.

Higher Leg Cut:

To redesign the leg opening, simply mark off the point on the hip that it will need to be cut up to, and:

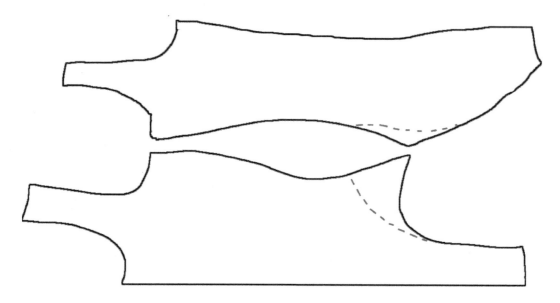

Front: Draw a curved line from the mark on the side seam, tapering in to where the leg opening straightens out towards the bottom/crotch seam. (Note: diagram shows a VERY high cut leg.)

Back: Draw a line that curves inward slightly from the mark on the side seam, and then goes fairly straight towards the leg seam, gradually curving into it. You don't want to remove a lot of the fullness in the butt part of the leotard, but you don't want to create bulging, either!

Lower Leg Cut / Boy Cut:

On both front and back pieces, extend the side seam, following the path it's on from the waist downward.

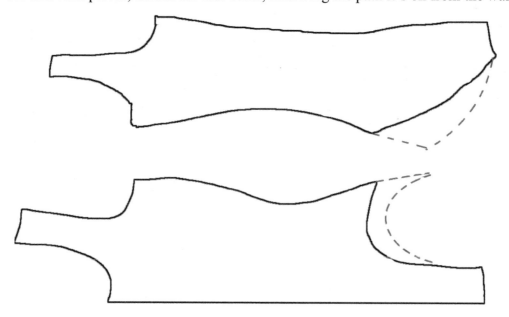

Mark off how long you want the additional side seam to extend, on both the front and back pieces.

Redraw the leg openings on both sides of the pattern, using the diagram on the previous page as a guide to how it should look.

"Wedgie Proofing"

I hated when my skating dresses would ride up, so I figured out this simple way of preventing the unpleasant situation. This is a simple alteration that you make to the back of the panty portion, before cutting your fabric. It works by "cupping" the butt with a little additional fabric.

Approximately halfway in between the end of the side seam and the corner of the crotch seam, mark a spot that is a few inches away from the pattern. Depending on the size of the gymnast, this should be between 1 inch and 2+ inches. The larger the gymnast, the further away.

Re draw the leg opening, starting about 1 inch inside the side seam, ending about 1 inch away from the crotch seam.

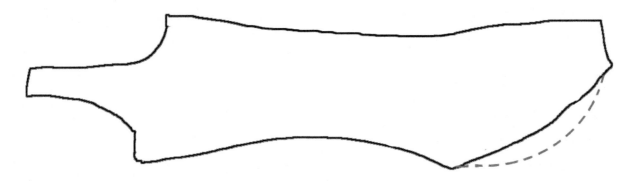

Adjusting the Skirt Line

Skirt placement lines are generally marked on all patterns, but usually are not very appropriate or flattering. For this reason, it's usually a good idea to get a pattern which has the bodice and panty all in one, so that you can tinker with the skirt placement.

Something to keep in mind: a pattern intended for a figure skating dress will have a very different skirt AND skirt placement than what you'll want for a rhythmic leotard. While skating skirts are placed fairly low and usually dip down in the front and back, rhythmic skirts are placed much higher - usually 4 to 4.5" above the top of the hip bone - and are fairly straight across.

While I was always a fan of "just winging it" - I could look at the gymnast, and know where to draw the skirt line on the pattern - those new to sewing for gymnasts will find it easiest to use a practice leotard to figure out skirt placement.

While your gymnast is wearing the properly fitting body suit, mark off where you would like the skirt line to be, on both the front and the back. (Hint: you really only need to make the skirt line on one half of the front, and one half of the back - no need to aim for a perfectly symmetrical skirt line across the entire front, or anything like that!).

Once you're satisfied with your marking, have the gymnast change out of the body suit, and transfer those markings to your well fitting body suit pattern. Along that line, make a note to yourself that you will need to add a little length for seam allowance to each side of the skirt line, when you cut it all out.

Base Pattern Alteration Final Notes

1.   You will likely find that commercially available patterns are sized too big for the standard gymnastics fit. Gymnasts tend to prefer a fit that is much tighter than the sizing assumptions made in commercial patterns. You may find that you'll end up making a size smaller than suggested, by default. Experiment!

2.   I recommend ALWAYS making a practice leotard from a pattern, before starting on a fancier or competition leotard - get the fitting right with cheaper fabric and less labour, before taking a risk on something more labour /cost intensive!

3.   Once you've got a basic pattern that fits - with folds, cuts, pen marks, new leg and butt seams, and all - trace the whole thing onto a fresh piece of paper. Behold! Your new master pattern!

4.   Assuming you've made a practice leotard from this new master pattern and are happy with everything, I recommend making a heavier copy - perhaps from craft paper - and setting it aside. Being able to trace that master pattern out onto a new sheet of tracing paper any time you need to make a new leotard will save you a lot of hassle!

5.   I reference Kwik-Sew patterns a lot, as that's what I recommended back in the day. Since that time, it seems that Jalie patterns have become very popular with gymnasts, and they even have a rhythmic leotard pattern available. While I can't specifically recommend them - I haven't used their gymnastics leotard patterns - I figure it's worth a look!

Sewing Techniques

In the Beginning

Before starting on the actual sewing of the leotard, make sure you have a few supplies on hand. Make sure that the needle in your sewing machine is a stretch sewing needle, suited to either light, medium, or heavy weight knits, depending on what you are using - and have extras on hand. For reference, regular spandex is a medium, illusion is a light, and stretch velvet is either a medium or heavy weight.

If you are using the metallic / foil spandex, you might want a Teflon foot on your machine. As far as thread goes, I prefer the Gutterman and Mettler brands for sewing with spandex... but that's largely a matter of personal preference.

Make sure that you have a sharp pair of scissors. Rotary cutters don't always work well with spandex, and dull scissors may pull your pieces out of shape as you are cutting, causing a distorted shape.

Cutting the Fabric

When selecting a print check the design, keeping in mind that the direction of greatest stretch has to go around the body. If there's a definite direction to the design, (for example, stripes) check to see which way it will lie on your body before you buy it. Do NOT try to swap the cutting directions, or the garment will not fit. (Ie. Don't try to cut a garment with the greatest degree of stretch going up and down, just because the pattern won't look as good going across.)

When cutting, lay out the pattern pieces with the fabric's greatest stretch going around the body. Use really sharp scissors. I once bought a pair of $60 industrial scissors.. they were an absolute dream to use! Dull scissors are a real headache to use. Rotary cutters can be great - but usually just for applique pieces. Use actual scissors for the main body, lining, etc. Never use rotary cutters for more than one layer of fabric at a time.

I tend to avoid using pins on spandex, but use them if you must. (For instance: When appliqueing onto mesh, definitely use pins.) The way I've always cut pieces out is by holding the fabric and pattern down with one hand, cutting with the other. If you do this, be very careful that you do not allow any of the fabric or pattern to move while you are cutting, or you will end up with a distorted piece of the garment.

A good way to get around using pins is to have a bunch of soup cans on hand, and lie them out on top of your pattern (after positioning it on the fabric). Move them around as you cut if they get in your way.

When cutting a piece of the pattern that requires two mirror-image pieces, fold the fabric in half and cut both layers at once. Things like the front suit piece, that have symmetrical halves, should be lined up with the centre edge along the fold of the fabric.

Some patterns of fabrics will have a definite one-way design. Make sure that you lay out all of your pieces facing the same way (have all of the upper portions (the shoulders) facing, for example, to the left.) If you don't do this, you will have part of the design going up, and part going down. As an example, say you have lengthwise arrows, and you don't take care to make the whole garment face the same way. You may end up with arrows pointing up in the front, and down in the back, as an example.

I cannot stress this enough: That is ALSO the way you *must* cut velvets! If you don't, any pieces that are cut facing different directions will look like completely different fabrics/colour when actually worn!

Also, - again! - whatever you do, just make sure that the greatest degree of stretch goes across the body. Trust me on this, and don't say I didn't warn you.

Seams

No matter what kind of machine you will be using, you will need to figure out your stitch options in order to get maximum amount of stretch in your seams. Be sure to practice on scrap pieces of fabric, stretching all practice seams - hard! - to make sure that they are durable. Seams should be more or less flat (some fabrics may ruffle slightly), and threads should not be puckering the fabric, or loose and loopy on one side.

I find the right side of the presser foot to be a great guide for seam allowances, on both traditional machines and sergers. When sewing any seam on spandex, hold the two pieces together, with the right sides facing each other (some exceptions apply).

Holding your edges together, sew along the side of fabric. As you are sewing, stretch the fabric. I usually hold the fabric in two places: my left hand is holding on to the garment BEHIND the sewing machine, the right hand is holding on to it in front of the machine.

Stretch the fabric in both directions (both pulling away from the machine), and hold it steady. You do not want to jerk the fabric, or pull it away from the machine in only one direction, or you run the risk of breaking the needle. Stretch it, and hold that degree of stretch throughout the seam. If you MUST release the stretch, stop the machine first. Adjust as needed and stretch - and HOLD - before starting the machine up again. You don't want to pull the fabric out from under the needle at all, just feed a tautly stretched span of fabric through.

A bit of a gory warning here: One time, I was sewing something ... and I guess I pulled the fabric too hard in one direction. The needle snapped in half. One side of the needle stayed in the machine, the other was still attached to the thread. Unfortunately, a third tiny piece decided to lodge itself into my eyeball. Having a doctor hunched over you, using a Q Tip to try and dislodge a tiny piece of metal out of your eye is NOT a pleasant experience. Needless to say, I can't see myself ever being able to wear contacts. The idea grosses me right out. Maintain your stretch!

Main body seams can be done in one of two ways: with a regular sewing machine, and with a serger. Whichever machine you choose, you'll want to follow the stretching technique described above, as you feed the fabric through.

Traditional Sewing Machine

First off - sergers may be great for sewing spandex, but if you don't have one, no worries - a regular sewing machine will work just fine, with the right technique.

Now, there are several different stitches you can choose to use. Your sewing machine might have a stretch stitch option, you may use a very narrow zig-zag, or a straight seam, among other possibilities. Different machines have different options, and it's all a matter of personal taste. I tend to use a plain straight seam, stretched.

At the starting point of your seam, sew a few stitches, then hit the reverse function and back over them. This acts as an anchor. Stretch the fabric as described above, and sew the seam.

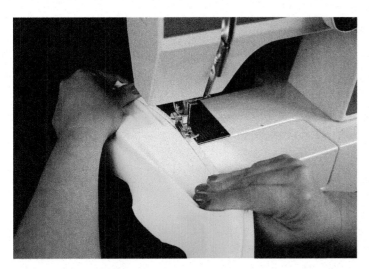

For zig zagging a finish to the seam, set your stitch width to be very wide. I usually like using the widest stitch possible. Your stitch length can be medium to long.

Stretch the fabric well, and sew a zig zag stitch as close as you can get to the edge, ideally going slightly over it.

The outer peaks of the zig zag should bind the edges of the fabric as it goes. Not only does this zig zag row add a little more strength to the seam, it finishes it and just plain looks better!

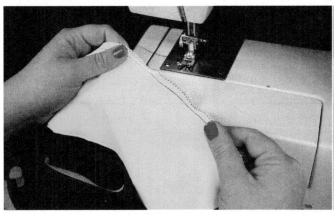

Standard sewing machines can easily produce strong, stretchy seams!

Sergers

Personally, I didn't like sergers for probably the first half of my sewing career. I convinced myself that it was because they made seams bulkier than they had to be, but really, I was just afraid of them, and HATED trying to thread them. This was back 20 years, though - today's sergers have become FAR more user friendly!

Rather than provide a set of instructions that may or may not apply to your serger, I highly recommend consulting your machine's user manual for advice on how to set it to serge stretch fabrics, and then play with it. Generally speaking, I set my differential feed to the highest number and use a medium stitch length for body seams (and a longer stitch length for elastic application)

I prefer to use a 4 thread, regular flat serger stitch. 3 thread overlock is another option, but you will likely want to use a regular sewing machine to sew a straight seam first, using the 3 thread serger to finish the seam - much as you would with the zigzag stitch described.

Whichever machine you have available, and whatever stitch you chose, just be sure to hold and stretch your fabric as described a bit earlier, and you'll be fine!

Elastic Application

You will need to apply elastic to all of the edges (openings) in order to keep the leotard in place. Most fabric stores will sell two main types of elastic:

Swimsuit elastic: This is the very thin, clear elastic. This isn't very strong, and if you aren't careful, you can shred it. The only thing I've ever really used swimsuit elastic on is when gathering edges for puffy sleeves on skating dresses. This elastic is clear and lightweight, so it doesn't add much in the way of bulk. I don't recommend using it for leg openings, etc. You may want to use it on neck/arm openings that involve unlined mesh or illusion, as well. (I don't tend to!)

Normal elastic. The stuff I prefer has a slightly fuzzy feel to it. It's really a matter of preference, get a feel for a few different types and brands, see what works for you. I know people who swear by swimsuit elastic, I don't. Do whatever works for you.

As far as "normal" elastic goes, there are two main quality types: "decent/good", and "don't bother". The way I tell the difference between the two is by stretching a length of the elastic. If you can see a grid-like pattern of square shaped holes, it's a cheap elastic, and doesn't have very good retention of stretch. If you stretch it, and don't see holes, it's probably a decent elastic. Don't buy anything that feels flimsy.

Generally speaking, I use 3/8" elastic for leg openings, necklines, arm holes, and straps, and either 3/8 or 3/4 inch for the under-bust shelf bra lining.

Leg Openings

I measure the amount of elastic to use right off the leotard. To do this, I lay the elastic down along the front leg opening, following the curve and being careful to only stretch it very slightly.

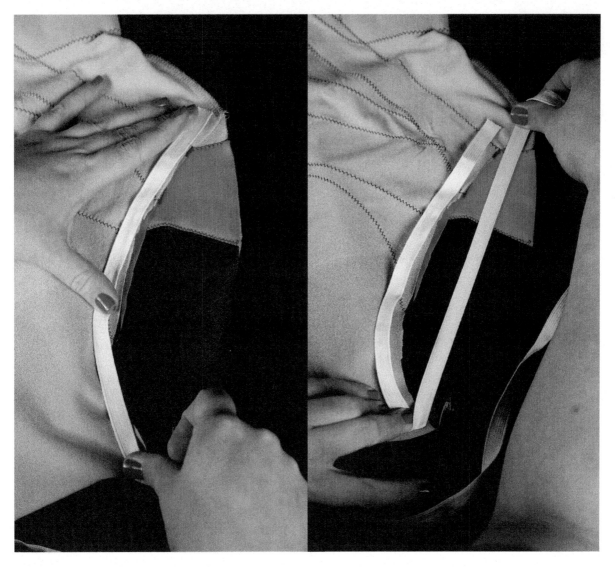

After getting the front measurement, I lay the elastic in a straight line from the bottom edge of the leg opening, to the side of the front leg opening. Cut two pieces of elastic at this length (front + back together).

If you'd like, sew one end of one of the pieces of elastic to the other end of itself. Be sure not to twist the elastic, it should make a continuous loop. Repeat for the other piece. Personally, I like to freehand it... but a loop can be easier for beginners to work with.

Lay the panty part at your sewing machine so that the front of it is being fed in, with the back piece behind the machine. The wrong side should be facing up. Line the elastic up with the edge of the fabric, and have your machine set to a wide and long zig zag stitch. Alternatively, use a serger set to a fairly long stitch length - pictured.

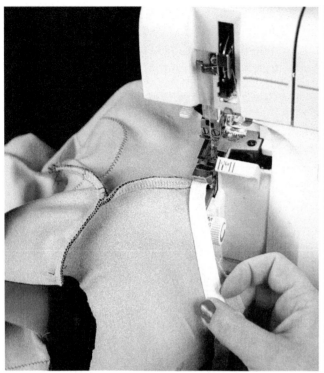
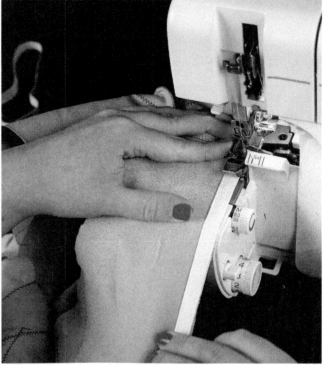

Sew the elastic to the front portion of the panty, (wrong side) stretching both pieces as you go. You should stretch the elastic ever so slightly more than the fabric, but stretch both well. Keep the elastic lined up with the side edge as you go.

When you get to the side seam, stop sewing, and straighten the elastic out so that it continues to lay across the leg opening. It will be much shorter than the actual fabric.

While firmly holding the elastic and leotard near where you stopped, stretch the upcoming section of leotard and

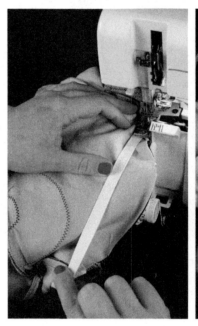
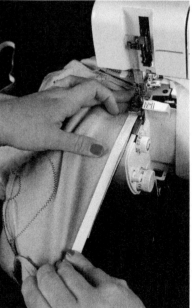

elastic together, till they match up. Find the approximate mid point of both the fabric and the elastic, and hold them together.

Sew from the side seam to the mid point, stretching the elastic to match up with the edge, and then some (the fabric should also be stretching, just not as much - proportionately - as the elastic.)

When you reach the mid point, you can let go of it, and grasp the original start point. Stretch the elastic and fabric once again, and sew the rest of the way around the leg opening.

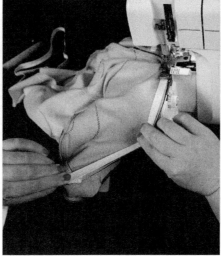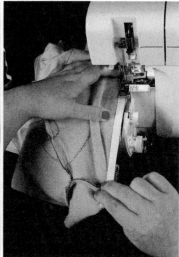

If you did not make a loop with the elastic before beginning, overlap the end of the elastic over the starting edge by about ½", stitch to secure. Cut the threads close to the fabric.

Turn the elastic over so that the exposed elastic is touching the wrong side of the fabric, and the underside of the seam you just did is facing up.

Sew another seam along the edge of the elastic (NOT the new edge of the opening). Stretch the garment as you sew this seam. This seam can be done in a wide or narrow zig zag (I don't like using straight stitches on an elastic). Personally, I like to use a very wide zig zag stitch, with a medium stitch length.

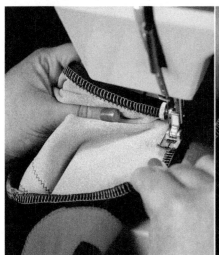

When sewing the second seam, try to make sure that the fabric does not bunch up and pucker under.

To avoid this, pull the garment fabric to the left as you sew, making sure that the fabric lies close to the elastic on the top, with no excess in the fold over. Don't worry if your stitching isn't perfect. The elastic will stretch and straighten out a bit when the leotard is worn, so imperfections are not all that noticeable. Practice makes perfect!

Alternatively, you can sew the flipped finishing seam with the leotard facing right side up - this is how I prefer to do it, and it's especially good for when you're dealing with changes of thread colour along the elastic seam.

Flip the elastic edge under, and position the leotard under your presser foot. Hold the back part of the leotard with your left hand, hook the fingers of your right hand under the upcoming part of the leotard, between the elastic and the leotard. Use those fingers to straighten everything out and pull the leotard fabric taut against the elastic as it feeds through your sewing machine. Stay stitch (reverse and then forward) at the beginning and end of each colour of thread used, switch colour of your top thread, and continue along.

Arm Holes

To measure the elastic needed for an arm hole, I like to take the distance between the seam (not the edge of fabric!) of the shoulder, and the side seam, in a straight line, then double it. This provides enough elastic to be comfortable, while retaining enough stretch to be secure when worn.

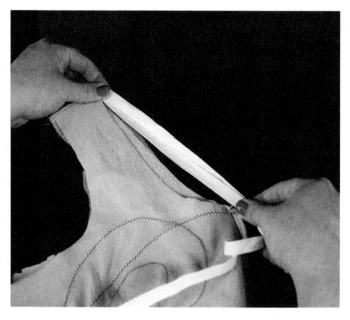

Applying elastic to the arm holes is very similar in technique to the leg opening application, with a small difference in where the stretch is applied.

I like to start all arm hole applications at the shoulder seam, but this is largely a matter of personal preference.

I look at the arm hole as two sections - the straightaways, and the curves. For the straightaways, apply a small amount of stretch to the elastic, before stretching elastic and fabric together to sew. The curved parts require a shorter amount of elastic, proportionately.

Fold your elastic in half, making note of where the halfway point is - a light mark with a pencil can be a great help, before you get comfortable enough to freehand it as you go. If you'd like to make a loop of it, as you may have with the leg, go ahead and do so. (Again, I prefer to freehand this part.)

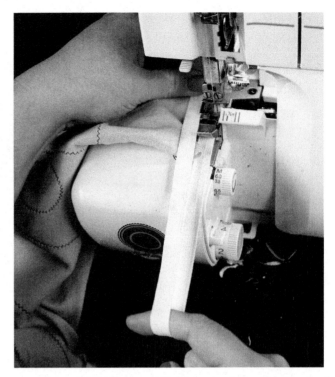

So, starting at the shoulder seam - with either the edge of a measured length of elastic, the seam of the loop, or the marked halfway point of a loop - line the elastic up with the upcoming straightaway. Stretch the elastic slightly to match a slightly longer length of fabric, holding the two together at a spot just before the armhole starts to curve out towards the side seam. Holding the fabric and elastic together both at that point and behind the needle, stretch it together, and sew the elastic on.

When you get to the point right before the curve, stop sewing. Line the next halfway point - the marked halfway point on either a loop or straightaway, or the seam of a loop if you started with the mark - with the side seam. Hold the fabric and elastic together, stretch, and continue to sew to that point. Make a mental note of how much elastic you had - before stretching - for the curved portion.

Once you come to the side seam, grasp a section of upcoming elastic at the approximate point away from the side seam, as your "mental note" measurement. If you stretched 2" of relaxed elastic to fit the curve on the first half of the armhole, this would be 2" away from the side seam, for example. Stretch that point of elastic to the point on your leotard where the curve straightens out to head back to the shoulder seam. Stretch everything together, sew to that point.

Stop sewing, line up the final stretch of elastic and leotard, match the edges up, stretch everything together, and sew the elastic down to the leotard. Finish off.

Flip the elastic and finish the edge as described for the leg elastic instructions.

Neck Holes

Neck hole elastic application is basically the same as arm hole application. Before applying elastic to the arm holes, measure the length of elastic needed for the neck hole.

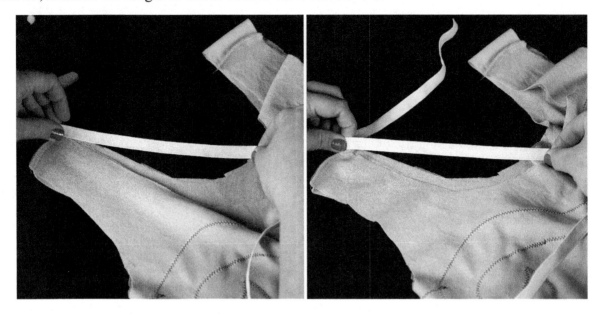

I like to take the distance between the seam (not the edge of fabric!) of the shoulder, and the center back seam, in a straight line. For the second part of the measurement, I measure from the shoulder seam to the center front of the leotard neckline. Combine these two measurements, and double that total. This provides enough elastic to be comfortable, while retaining enough stretch to be secure when worn.

Like the arm holes, the neckline has two types of sections - the straightaways, and the curves. For the straightaways, apply a small amount of stretch to the elastic, before stretching elastic and fabric together to sew. The curved parts require a shorter amount of elastic, proportionately.

I like to start all neckline elastic applications at the shoulder seam and freehand the measurements from there, but this is largely a matter of experience + personal preference. For beginners, it's usually easier to start at the center back seam.

Fold your elastic in half, making note of where the halfway point is - a light mark with a pencil can be a great help, before you get comfortable enough to freehand it as you go. If you'd like to make a loop of it, as you may have with the leg, go ahead and do so. (Again, I prefer to freehand this part.)

So, starting at the center back seam - with either the edge of a measured length of elastic, the seam of the loop, or the marked halfway point of a loop, make a few stitches to secure the elastic to the leotard at that point.

Without allowing the elastic to twist around, hold the halfway point of the elastic to the center front of the leotard. With everything stretched together relatively flat, make not of where the elastic meets up with the first shoulder seam. Pin or mark that spot on the elastic. Mark another spot the same distance from the halfway point, but on the other side of the halfway point.

For example, if the shoulder seam mark is 6" away from the halfway point (when not stretched), mark a spot 6" away from the halfway point on the OTHER side of it.

Depending on the style of your neckline, your elastic may or may not be divided up into 3 equal measurements. If not, it will be divided into 2 sets of equal measurements.

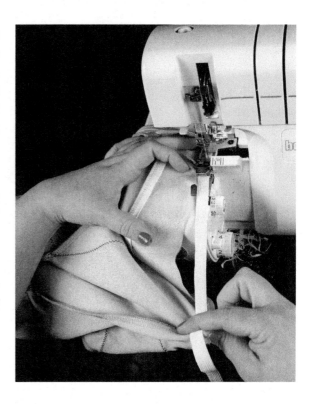

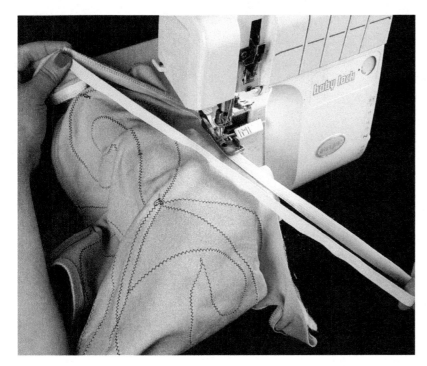

Using your best judgement and the technique for the arm holes, sew the elastic on. Stretch the elastic a bit more on the curves (center back and center front), and a bit less on the straightaways. Use the marks for the shoulder and center front spots to determine how much elastic you have to work with for a particular section of leotard.

Once you're coming up on the end of the elastic, line up the final stretch of elastic and leotard, match the edges up, stretch everything together, and sew the elastic down to the leotard. Finish off.

Flip the elastic and finish the edge as described for the leg elastic instructions.

Thread Colour Selection

Generally speaking, if there is any mesh involved at all, I will sew all of the side seams with white or beige thread.

If the leotard is a solid colour - no mesh - I will sew the seams with that colour.

If the leotard is solid spandex, but in various colours, I'll sew the side seams to match the either the lightest colour of spandex used, or something in the mid range - it's a judgement call.

Once you've sewn the side (structural) seams, flip the leotard right side out, and examine the seams. If the seam is really obvious due to the colours used, you'll want to go over sections of seam with a plain straight stitch, in a more appropriate colour.

For example: The main part of the leotard is black, but beige mesh was used in some parts, so the seams were sewn in white/beige. When opened up, the white/beige could show up in between sections of black.

Should this happen, simply use a regular sewing machine to stitch a straight seam - in a more appropriate colour - - in the sections that need it. Stay stitch on either side of the new seam - stretching as you go - and keep it very close to the original seam - just slightly further away from the garment edge.

When it comes to multiple colours - beige mesh excluded - on elasticized leotard openings, exercise your best judgement. If you have several colours that are "close enough", I wouldn't both changing the colour of thread as you zig zag the elastic seam over. For instance, if you have hot pink and a bright orange, no one will see the hot pink thread against the orange from more than a foot away.

Always finish elastic seams in meshed areas with thread to match the mesh. You really want these sections to disappear against the skin as much as possible.

Note: you'll notice that the thread colour selections in the photos throughout this book will not necessarily match what is being said here. In the interest of showing the stitches/ techniques, we have elected to use wildly inappropriate thread colour choices! For thread colour, ignore the photos, and follow this section's recommendations instead!

Colour Blocking

Colour blocking adds interest to a garment by breaking it up into different sections of colours. It's also a great way to make use of leftover fabric from other projects. (Note: you will see this technique used mostly for practice leotards and in artistic gymnastics leotards, mens singlets, etc ... not so much in rhythmic competition leotards, though.)

Colour blocking is a lot like quilting. You can have as many pieces as you want, just keep in mind that you will be sewing them back together. Start simple, it can get confusing.

Decide on a design for the garment. On the actual pattern (or a tracing thereof), mark the lines of your design. If your design is not symmetrical, you will need a full pattern, not just the half-pattern pieces that you'd work with for symmetrical leotards. Fold a piece of paper in half, trace the pattern half out, using the fold as the centre edge, and cut it out.

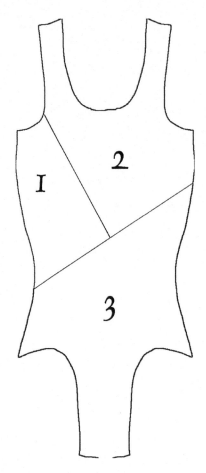

In case of confusion, label each piece of the pattern as being "right side up", and draw a little sketch if you need to, to remind you which piece goes where. Also, mark a line straight across each pattern piece as it lays as a full pattern. This will be your guide to make sure that you have the greatest degree of stretch going across the body. I must sound like a nag by now, but it really IS that important.

Along every new line you draw, run a highlighter, or make a scribble with a pen. This will show you which edges you will need to add a seam allowance to.

Cut the pattern apart, and position it on the various pieces of fabric. Add a 1/4 inch seam allowance to each of the new edges that you created. If the edge already existed, such as it being a side seam, waist line, etc, do not add a seam allowance. Make sure that you pay attention to the greatest degree of stretch - keeping it going straight across the body - and that the right sides match up.

Lay the fabric pieces out to approximate what the garment will look like, with all "right" sides of the fabric facing up. Now is when you will decide which seams to sew first. If the colour blocking is simple, such as stripes, or just a garment divided in half, this will be pretty obvious. If the design is more complicated, you will need to plan ahead to take the path of least headaches.

For instance, if your garment is one colour on the bottom half, and the top half is split into 2 different colours, you would sew the seam between the two upper colours first, then sew the bottom half on to it. Practice makes perfect. Attaching smaller pieces together to form a block or panel which will then match up with either another panel, or a longer edge is a lot easier than, say, trying to piece a squared edge into an L shaped opening.

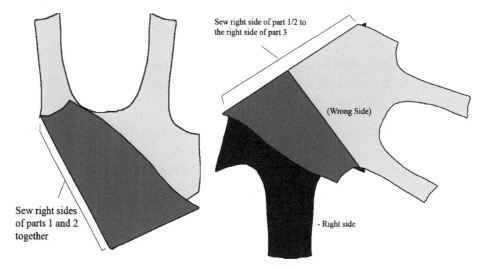

Sew right side of part 1/2 to the right side of part 3

(Wrong Side)

Sew right sides of parts 1 and 2 together

- Right side

Applique

Applique is a great way to add colour and design interest to a garment, without the need to be as basic and blocky as colour blocking. It's especially good for complicated shapes, overlapping, etc... and is how MOST large colour-based design effects are created. When you see multiple colours of fabric making up a design on a leotard... odds are, you're looking at applique.

First, let's look at applique on the absolute more basic level - sewing one piece of fabric onto another. There are two main ways to accomplish this - regular applique, and reverse applique. Both make use of my secret tool for applique - 3M Spray Mount.

Before getting started on applique, I highly recommend using Spray Mount to create a "sticky paper" work surface. I swear, this will make your life SO much easier, as you get going with applique!

To do so, cut out a big piece of craft paper, bristol board, or rosin paper (Rosin paper can be found at hardware/lumber stores, and is also great for making "master" patterns!)

Spray a thin coat of Spray Mount all over the center of your work space sheet, avoiding the edges. You don't want to spray right off the edge of the paper, as it can be a pain to clean off of other surfaces. Allow to dry for about 5 minutes (it will still be tacky), and you're ready to go! More on Spray Mount in a bit...

"Regular" Applique.

(Note: When I refer to "applique" throughout this book, I am generally referring to this style).

Regular applique occurs when you cut a shape out of one piece of fabric, and stitch it down to the surface of another piece of fabric. For example, let's look at a basic leaf shape, cut from lime green hologram print spandex.

Cut your desired shape out of the desired fabric, place it face down in the middle of your sticky paper.

Spray lightly with Spray Mount adhesive, allow to dry for 30 seconds or so.

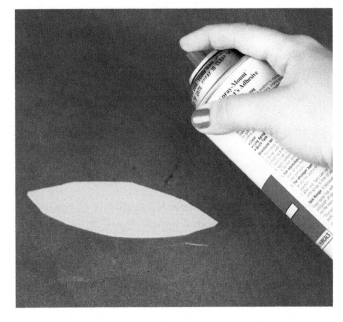

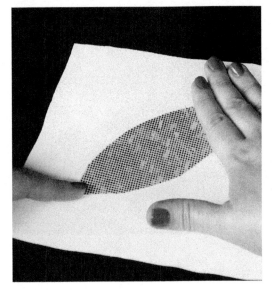

Lay the piece out - right side up - on the desired location of the actual garment. Smooth any wrinkles out, and press firmly to secure the applique to the main fabric.

Note: Even with the Spray Mount, you may end up wanting to pin certain applique fabrics in a few areas. For instance, appliqueing anything onto mesh can usually use a few pins! When pinning, be very careful to keep the garment flat, not allowing for any bunching.

Thread your machine with thread to match the applique (not the garment), and set your stitch to be a wide zig zag, with a medium stitch length. Play around with your settings to see what you prefer.

Carefully zig zag around the applique, stretching both layers together as you go. Keep your zig zag VERY close to the edge of the applique, and be very careful that nothing puckers or bunches.

When you reach the start point of your stitching, back stitch a few times, then forward a few stitches. Trim thread close to the applique.

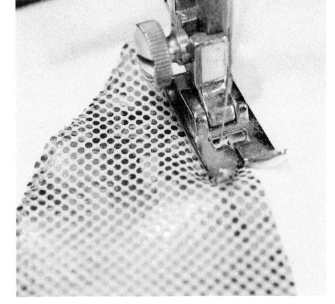

Reverse Applique

Reverse applique occurs when you cut a shape out of a main piece of fabric, position a contrasting fabric underneath it, and stitch around the edge of the main piece. This technique is great for when your contrasting design is lighter than the main body of the leotard.

As an example: You have a black leotard, and want to applique a pale yellow design on. Using standard applique, there is a good chance that the black will show through the yellow, making it appear darker or even muddy. Much better to cut the design out of the black, and stitch the yellow behind it.

Another reason to use reverse applique is when the main body fabric is highly textured, to the point where it would show through a lighter-fabric applique. As an example - main body of leotard is white, but printed with hologram dots. You want to applique a pale yellow onto it. While white won't show through the yellow on its own, the texture of the hologram could.

As a working example, let's look at a basic leaf shape, cut from lime green hologram print spandex. The appliqued design will be in yellow, behind the cutout.

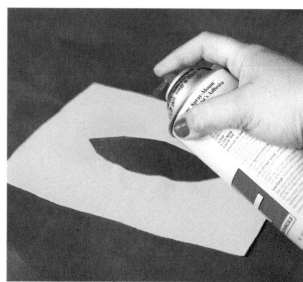

Cut your desired shape out of the main piece of fabric. Place this main piece face down in the middle of your sticky paper.

Lightly spray around the edge of the cutout with Spray Mount adhesive, allow to dry for 30 seconds or so.

Lay the piece out - right side up - on the desired location of the actual garment. Smooth any wrinkles out, and press firmly to secure the applique to the main fabric.

Note: Even with the Spray Mount, you may end up wanting to pin certain applique fabrics in a few areas. For instance, appliqueing anything onto mesh can usually use a few pins! When pinning, be very careful to keep the garment flat, not allowing for any bunching.

Thread your machine with thread to match the main body of the garment (not colour going underneath), and set your stitch to be a wide zig zag, with a medium stitch length. Play around with your settings to see what you prefer.

Carefully zig zag around the applique, stretching slightly as you go. Be very careful that nothing puckers or bunches. Keep your zig zag VERY close to the edge of the applique.

When you reach the start point of your stitching, back stitch a few times, then forward a few stitches. Trim thread close to the applique.

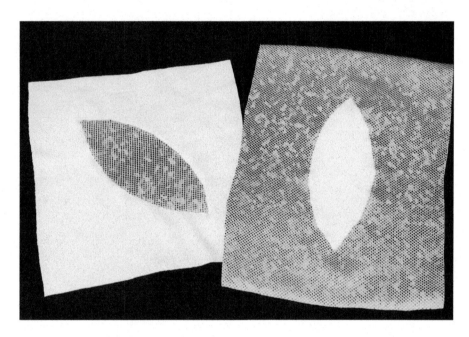

Regular applique on the left, reverse applique on the right

So, there you have it - applique in its two most basic forms. Now... let's have some fun with it.

Applique From Printed Fabric

Feeling a little lazy? Cut your appliques out from pre printed fabric! As an example, floral print fabrics are perfect for this... this works particularly well for rhythmic leotards.

Just cut your desired applique out of the fabric, lay it face down on your sticky paper, and spray.

Lay your applique out on the appropriate section of leotard body, and proceed as you would with a basic regular applique!

Looking do so something more elaborate than a simple leaf or flower? Let's continue. First, a bit more information, and a few simple tools will help you out...

Paper

When I started out with spandex costuming, I went through a lot of newspapers (messy and inconvenient), and brown craft paper (which got expensive, and presented its own problems). Let me explain further, so that you don't need to repeat my mistakes!

Newspaper: There were a few problems with this. Size was sometimes an issue, and I'd have to tape lengths of newspaper pages together to say, do a full length applique for tights. Also, newspaper tears far too easily for complicated applique.

The biggest problem with newspaper is the transfer of inks. Where adhesives are used with my applique technique, it's just not a good idea to use paper with ink that will rub off. Even for appliques without the use of adhesives, there's still the worry of general rub off - the inks can get on your fingers, and will make lighter fabrics look awful. You know, unless you're going for a CSI theme, and *want* fingerprints all over your finished product!

Brown Craft Paper: I'd buy this on rolls at Staples / Business Depot. The two main problems were opacity and paper thickness. Being able to see through your pattern paper comes in really handy, and you don't get that property in craft paper. Paper thickness is an issue for 2 reasons: It makes it more difficult to cut intricate designs, and wears down your scissors. Because you want really sharp scissors for cutting your designs, this is a really bad thing!

The solution?   Medical exam-table paper.

You can buy rolls of this at medical supply stores, for between $2-5 per roll. Super cheap - which is good, because you'll go through it like crazy once you get going! Usually you'll be given a choice of 2 papers. One is cheaper and uncoated, and the other is slightly more expensive, and is coated. Go for the cheaper roll. If you do this as a business, you'd be best off to buy it by the case - usually 21-24 rolls. Exam table paper is ideal for a few reasons.

- It cuts easily, and doesn't ruin scissors. (Though I still like to use "paper-designated" scissors for it)

- It's sheer, making it perfect for tracing, making layered appliques, etc.

- It's cheap. If you screw up, use some more. No big deal!

- The roll size is convenient.

- It's not a fad product. I'm sure we've all come across some gadget marketed to make our lives easier, then disappears, leaving you wondering what to use as a suitable replacement.

- No inks or dyes!

I used exam table paper for all of my base patterns, as well as appliques. Sometimes, I have up to 5 complete patterns for 1 leotard, based on the applique and layering. Exam table paper makes it all really easy!

Pens/Markers

Don't bother with pencils - ideally, you shouldn't erase on the paper, just cross out / redraw / start again. If you are working with white or light Spandex... be very, very careful, and make sure you know where your pens / markers / marked applique pieces are at ALL times!

Spray Adhesive:

There are 3 main brands / types of spray adhesive that are in any way suitable for spandex costuming. One of the 3 is ideal. One of the 3 is a case of "use it if you have to, if you're experienced and patient". The third is more a case of "If you're absolutely desperate, and not too concerned with imperfections that show".

The first is the aforementioned product by 3M, called "Spray Mount". Love it. This will fast become your best friend, and if you do a lot of applique, you'll want to buy it by the case. Basically, this spray will turn your applique - or pattern - into a post it note. One important quality it has is that it does NOT soak though. It's also easily repositioned, without leaving residue. As I write this, I get portions of the "How do I love thee" sonnet stuck in my head. It *IS* that good!

The second product is also by 3M, called "Super 77 Adhesive Spray". This has a low amount of soak through - just make sure you don't spray too heavily, or too close to the surface being sprayed. The main problem with Super 77 is that it is FAR more permanent than Spray Mount. If you are experienced, fairly accurate at placing applique, and aren't doing anything super complicated.. this should work fine for you. If you spray the back of a complex applique with this, be prepared to spend some time straightening it out - it will has a tendency to stick to itself, and will become incredibly annoying within a short amount of time.

The third product is Elmer's Spray Glue. This has a high rate of soak through - you can get permanent spotting on the fabric - and it doesn't really hold well. It's about ½ - 1/3 the price of the other two, but in this case, you really do get what you pay for.

You can find these spray adhesives in the craft section of stores like Staples and Office Depot, or in the painting section of stores like Walmart (with the stencilling stuff). Look for a spray can that give instructions "for a temporary bond..."

Glue Sticks

While glue sticks (I always liked the UHU brand best) are too cumbersome to use on complicated appliques, they are VERY handy for sticking a spandex applique to mesh - something that the spray adhesive isn't the best at. Lightly dab along the edge (not drag!), position, press, and allow to FULLY dry before sewing.

Rulers & Other Guides

For accuracy, and help in positioning, it's good to have a ruler or two on hand. Other things you can have on hand include french curves, and/or those bendable blue curves for creating your own shape guides, protractors, compasses, etc. Also, things around the house. Different size plates and glasses are great for circles, etc. Improvise whenever you need to! Looking for something very specific? Google is your friend. Find an image, size it with photo editing software, and print out your applique pattern!

Special Fabric Considerations

Certain fabrics will work for appliques, but require a little bit of special treatment to do so.

- Anything appliqued onto mesh will likely need to be pinned down in addition to sprayed. (Or use glue stick!). This is particularly important for rhythmic leotards, which make extensive use of mesh.

- Foil/metallic Spandex may require a Teflon foot. Such fabrics can be a little "sticky", causing them to drag and bunch as they catch on the bottom of the sewing foot.

- 4 way stretch PVC works well for applique... not so much for the main body of the leotard. You CAN use it, but be aware that the plastic coating can pull/lift at the seams. When using PVC, be sure to use a Teflon foot.

- No Teflon foot? No problem! Go to a dollar store and find the cheapest hand lotion you can find - the really greasy stuff. Lightly swipe a very thin coat of this over your PVC or foil areas, and sew as usual. Be sure to wipe it off as soon as possible, or it could discolour. Also, it's usually a good idea to test this on scraps of fabric before actually doing it on a leotard, in case your particular lotion or fabric has issues.

Designing Your Applique

After you have a well sized base pattern ("Pattern Alterations"), use it to make a blank leotard pattern to work with. If your leotard is symmetrical, you can use a half pattern. For the sake of illustration, we'll use an asymmetrical bodysuit design to demonstrate - the principle works the same for bodices, tights, whatever.

If your leotard is not symmetrical, cut your working pattern out of a folded piece of paper, lining the fold up with the center of the front of the leotard pattern. Additionally, you will want to cut two copies of the back of your leotard pattern.

Draw your overall design out onto your pattern, using a marker. If you need to redraw a line of the design, just scribble over the line to remind yourself to not use it.

Where designs extend from front to back, line up your pattern pieces to make sure the pattern will continue over as you want it to. Remember to account for the seam allowance on either side of the pattern - especially in the case of appliques that extend across the seam at an angle. After you make a few leotards, this will all become instinctual!

Once you're happy with your front and back designs - individually, and how they match up together - it's time to make the patterns for individual applique pieces.

Use a new piece of exam table paper, and trace over each design element individually. Leave enough space around each pattern piece to make it easier to cut the pieces out. Also, as you trace each individual piece, be sure to write the colour on it. Not only will this keep the colours straight, it will identify which side of your pattern is "right side up". This will be important, later!

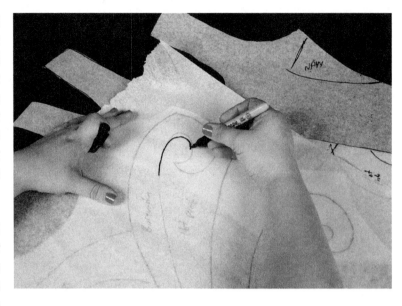

If you have any mesh to your design, you'll not only need to make pattern pieces for the "design" applique pieces, but the coloured "body" piece of your leotard, as well. It will essentially act as a large applique, itself! (Note: In the example shown here, we utilize a full lining on the leotard, rather than requiring a separate liner. You don't need to line your leotard - the main body being appliqued onto can be mesh or lycra instead!

Cutting Applique Pieces

You know how I swear by Spray Mount for appliqueing fabric? Well, it also makes life easier when it comes to cutting the appliques in the first place! Basically, the stuff lets you make a post-it note out of your pattern... which you can then apply to your fabric, making cutting easier.

Especially you have a really complex applique - such as a panel of hotrod style flames - it really helps with cutting the fabric. No pins necessary!

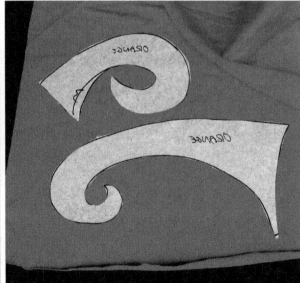

Spray the RIGHT SIDE of the pattern, wait 30 seconds, then position it face down on the wrong side of the fabric.

52

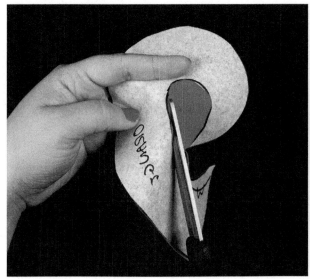 

Cut the applique piece out, and peel the paper off. Very easy! Repeat with remaining colours and pieces.

Once you have all of your applique pieces cut out, all you have to do is spray the WRONG side of the fabric, and position it on the garment where you want it, and proceed with zig zagging the edges, as a regular applique!

Layering Appliques

When overlapping appliques over other appliques, you may want to trim the excess fabric out from underneath each respective layer, as you go. Good thing that Spray Mount is repositionable - just make note of where you can remove bulk from, lift the outermost layer, trim back the layer beneath, and reposition the upper layer.

Alternatively, when you become confident with your accuracy in placing the more complicated applique pieces, you can just cut your applique patterns in a way to reduce as much bulk as possible. As an example, on the next page are some progress photos of a "Firebird Suite" synchro swim suit that I designed, back in the day. Each colour is stitched down before the next colour is appliqued over top.

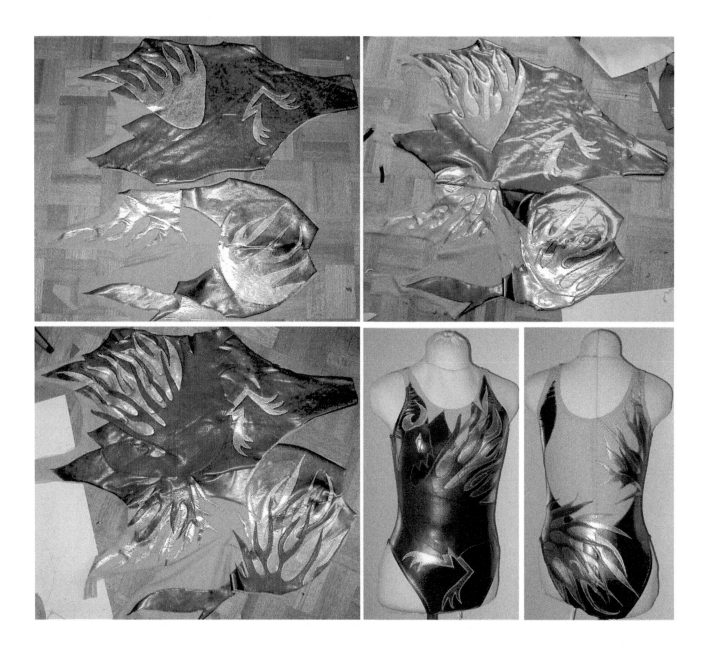

Lace Overlays

Looking for a quick way to achieve a customized textural look? Spray the right side of a section of regular spandex with Spray Mount, allow to dry for 30 seconds or so.

Smooth this out onto the wrong side of a larger piece of 4 way stretch lace. Trim the excess lace, and proceed - either as an applique, or a main body piece of fabric. Try red spandex under black lace for a "Spanish" look, or any high contrast mix of spandex and lace. Bright turquoise under black, pastels under white... whatever!

Piping

Piping is a way to emphasize a seam, whether to just to add a little emphasis to it (same colour as the rest of the body of the garment), or to bring another colour to the leotard. It can be used to as a outline between sections of colour blocking, and can bring a little "something" to a simple leo.

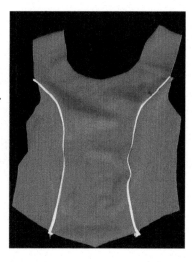

Although it is most commonly used in colour blocked seams, piping can be added to any seam. Keep in mind that the piping needs to stretch as much as the rest of the garment! An average finished piping, once set into the seam, is about 1/8 inch wide. To do this:

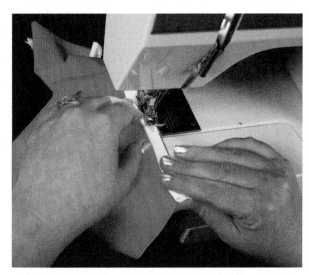

Cut a strip of Lycra that is 3/4 in. wide by the length of the seam, with the direction of greatest stretch running lengthwise. (Short end to short end)

Fold the piping in half, wrong sides together, and zigzag along the long edge. You should use a wide, loose basting-type zigzag for this. If you're confident at your coordination, you can skip this step. (I do)

Zigzag the edge of your piping in place on the good side of one piece of the two that will make up your intended seam. The raw edges of the piping should be matched up to the edge of that piece of the garment, with the folded edge inward.

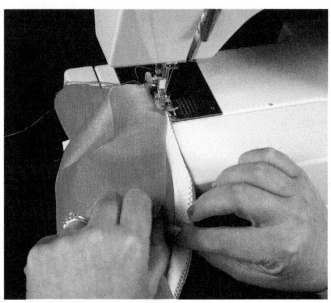

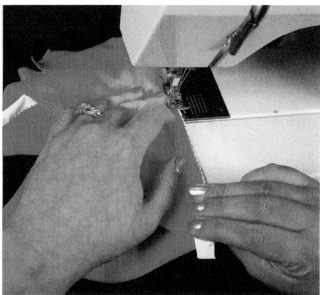

Sandwich this piping into the seam, with the right sides of the two main body pieces of fabric facing each other. Sew a regular straight seam, with a 1/4 inch seam allowance. Finish the seam as usual - zig zag or serger.

Lining

Generally speaking, leotards do not require a lining. Gymnasts will wear them as-is, or with a separate, purchased liner garment.

If the leotard is white, really pale, or the fabric is really sheer (Some spandex is thinner than others), it's a good idea to have some sort of a lining, rather as a separate garment, or a built in lining. For these leotards, I really prefer to build in the lining - it just allows for a stronger, more durable leotard. Also, lining provides a great base structural layer for appliqueing, especially in the case of very mesh-y rhythmic leotards.

When lining a leotard, look for a good quality swimsuit lining (usually beige). Beige swimsuit lining gives the most professional looking end product, especially when lighter colours and/or mesh are involved.

There are two main ways to line a garment : separate, and built on.

For a separate lining, you would sew the lining as you would the rest of the leotard - all of the "good" sides together, with additional seams at the crotch and shoulders. The lining is positioned inside the outer body of the leotard - good side of the outer leotard facing out, good side of the lining facing inward, and the seams of each facing each other. The pieces are held or otherwise tacked together, and the elastic is applied to each leotard opening (neck, legs, etc), sewing through both layers of fabric.

It really is that simple, but there's another reason for glossing over it a bit - it's really not a great technique for building a leotard. Using this technique is great for undecorated leotards, but doesn't give the structure and stability that I like for working with appliques. May as well save the effort and buy a liner, in this case.

SO, for appliqued leotards: Cut your lining pieces from your original, size-adjusted pattern - the same base pattern that you end up marking up for applique. Lay them out flat on your work surface- a table, or the floor if you need more space - and build on it.

Layer by layer, spray your outer leotard pieces, and smooth them out on your lining. If you have any mesh, make sure that goes on first, and is cut big enough to extend beyond where it actually needs to go. If you have several areas of mesh, just cut a large piece, even almost the entire pattern size if needed. Smooth everything out and press down as you go.

When each piece of your leotard has been stitched for the applique, sew the main body seams, stitching through all layers of lining and outer fabric. Your lining is now completely built in, and will not move or bunch as the gymnast moves.

Shelf Bra Lining

The one lining that shouldn't be built in before doing your applique work is a shelf bra type lining. You won't need to do these often: only if a gymnast has a particularly large chest, or a leotard is extra sheer, and you want a little more modesty protection. I loved this method when I was a figure skater, because I would always get overheated and needed big open backs in my skating outfits. I was too "endowed" to just get away with going braless in a store bought dress.

Anyway, to make a shelf bra lining:

From the same pattern you are using for the front of your leotard (all neckline and other adjustments already made), trace out a short "bra" piece. This should resemble a sports bra, and be long enough to just fit under the breasts. If it is too long, your gymnast could look saggy, and if it is not long enough, she may fall out the bottom. From personal experience, I can tell you that falling out of the bottom is rather awkward! Look to a reliable sports bra for an idea of how long you should cut the pattern.

Trim the shoulder straps off of the leotard - the lining will just add bulk to shoulder straps - and use the new pattern to cut a piece out from swimsuit lining.

Cut a piece of elastic (3/8" is a good width, pick an elastic with a good strong feel to it - wussy elastic just won't do!) that is about ½" shorter than the bottom edge of the lining piece. Zig Zag the elastic to the lining, making sure to stretch the elastic to fit, as well as stretch both the elastic and the lining together.

With the elastic side facing up, lay the lining on top of the front leotard piece - AFTER all applique is finished, if applicable.

Line up the bra piece with the body piece, zig zag the lining to the leotard, following along the short sides, arm holes, shoulders, and neckline. From this point, sew the garment as usual. (If you're confident in your skills, you can skip the zig zagging and just sew the bra in as a third layer when sewing the main body seams)

For a more visual idea of what you're looking at doing:

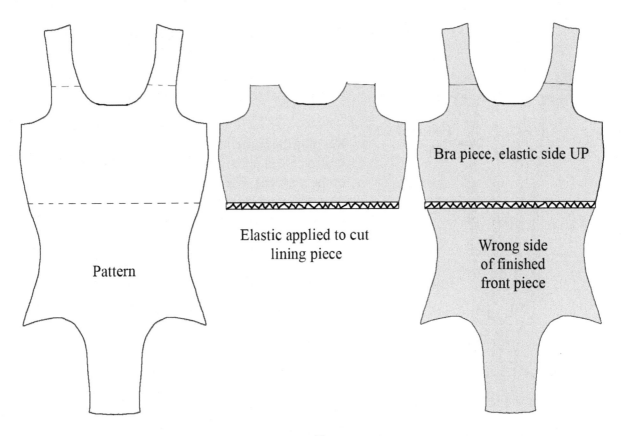

Pattern

Elastic applied to cut lining piece

Bra piece, elastic side UP

Wrong side of finished front piece

Zippers

Let me repeat what I said in the "Functionality" section, as it can't be stressed strongly enough:

"Zippers can be a touchy issue. Personally, I have no use for them. The thing with zippers is that they were not intended to be used on stretch fabrics in the first place, and every time you add something like a zipper into a seam, that is introducing a point of weakness to the garment. As a bit of trivia, many professional ballet dancers (I've been told Russian ballet dancers in particular) don't even use zippers in their costumes, they are sewn in to them.

I'd be willing to bet that most, if not all "performance athletes" (Figure skaters, gymnasts, synchro swimmers, etc) have either busted a zipper, seen someone bust a zipper, or heard a story about someone busting a zipper in competition. Aside from the fact that a zipper busting is very embarrassing and a hassle, even just having a zipper can add worry to an athlete's mind during the competition. As stress can negatively impact performance, I find it best to just steer clear of zippers. "I hope my zipper doesn't break", as a stress, can be avoided by not having one to worry about - leaves more time to worry about sticking that landing!"

If you can at all avoid having one in your leotard... avoid it. In addition to being incredibly easy to bust, zippers are also a pain in the butt to sew into spandex.

An invisible zipper is inserted in an entirely open seam; the rest of the seam is stitched after the application is completed. A zipper foot is really handy for this, but if you are brave, you can go without. Have extra zippers on hand, just in case.

Before starting, press the zipper as follows, using a synthetic setting: Open zipper; from wrong side, press zipper flat, using point of iron to push coil over so that the two rows of stitching show. I hear this works, but I'm a purist - I just do it manually, holding it open as I go.

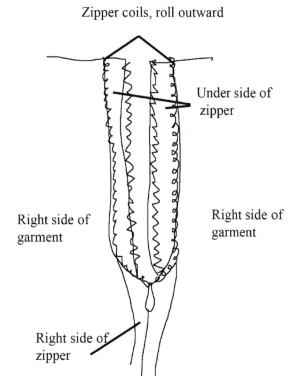

Zipper coils, roll outward

Under side of zipper

Right side of garment

Right side of garment

Right side of zipper

Keeping the garment flat, and being VERY CAREFUL not to stretch it at all, zig zag the edge of the zipper to the edge of the garment. The top edge of the zipper should be lined up with the top edge of the garment, with the outside of the zipper face down on the right side of the garment.

Attach the invisible zipper foot to the machine, with the needle lined up with center mark/groove. Pin zipper in place and sew from the top edge of the garment downward. Stitch zipper until you reach the end of the zipper, or the final length you'd like the opening to be, if shorter than the actual zipper. Remove pins as you come to them. Trim thread at the end

(If not ironing: Open the zipper, and lie one edge flat against one of the sides of the garment, where you will be applying the zipper. The zipper will be attached to the RIGHT side of the fabric. The coil edge of the zipper should be facing up, and away from the edge of the fabric. As you sew the straight seam later, you should flip the coil over as you go.)

To attach the other half of the zipper, pin the zipper with the coil on the upper side and on seam line (5/8" in). Zig zag into place, having the top edge lined up with the top edge of the garment, as before. Make sure that the zipper is not twisted at the bottom. Use the left-hand groove of foot, making sure that the center marking is still lined up with the needle and stitch, as before.

Close zipper. Pin the seam together below zipper opening. Fold end of zipper out of the way. Sew your seam from the zipper downward, starting slightly above and to the left of the last stitch. Stitch seam for about 2". End your seam here, and tie off. Change to regular foot and complete the seam .

NB: My best piece of advice about invisible zippers is this: your sanity is more important than a zipper. I've been doing this for 22 years, and have always had an easy time applying these zippers to bridal and formalwear. When it comes to leotards? I can't think of anything more aggravating!

Closures

There are 5 main types of closures that are used for spandex costuming: snap, velcro, hook-and-eye, swimsuit hook, and butterfly snap,

Snap Closures

I find these to be the weakest, and the easiest to pop open while moving. Personally, I tend to avoid them. If the gymnast in question is small, and not very hard on their leotards, snap closures will work just fine. Snap closures require an end allowance just slightly larger than the diameter of the snap itself. Metal snaps are much better than the clear plastic ones. To attach them:

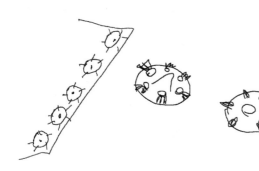

Stitch one half of a closure to the right side of the opening that you intend to close. If the edge of the opening is wide, add a row of a few more. To stitch it in place, run a thread (with one end knotted to secure) down through the fabric in the place you would like the snap. Pull back up through the fabric, and thread through one of the holes in the snap. Bring back down through the fabric, and repeat along all the other holes. You might want to do this several times for each hole, for strength. When you are confident that your snap will not fall off, knot the end of the fabric well, and trim the end of the thread.

Hold the two edge pieces together so that they overlap, with the snaps sandwiched in between. On the side that has no snaps on it yet, mark the positions that you will be applying the other half of the snaps.

Sew the opposite sides of the snaps to the marked edge of the other opening. Take special care to make sure that the snaps line up, and are sewn so that they will actually close (don't sew any pieces in backwards).

Velcro Closure

This was one of two of my favourite closures for turtle necks on practice dresses, back in the day. It's not often seen in gymnastics leotards, though - but works very well for young kids. The only downfall is that it should not be used if the closure will be under very high stress (halter tops for very top-heavy girls, for instance). This closure should NOT be used on illusion, as it will catch on it and ruin the fabric.

Velcro can be bought both with and without a sticky backing to it. The sticky backing is nice because it will secure it to the fabric as you sew, so you don't have to worry about pinning it down.

Make sure that you include an extra bit of allowance on one side of the edge you will be closing, that is the same width as the velcro. I like the 1 inch velcro. Cut a piece that is as long as the edge that you will be closing.

Secure the "hook" side of the velcro to the edge that will be facing up. If you have the hook side facing down, it has a higher possibility of catching on the fabric as you fumble to do it up.

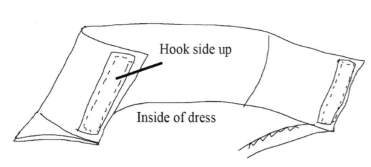

Hook side up

Inside of dress

Sew a straight seam around the outside of the piece of velcro. Finish the seam with a few reverse stitches, and trim the thread.

Position the "soft" side of the velcro on the edge of the fabric that will be overlapping the "hook" side. Line up the two pieces of velcro, and secure the "soft" side to the fabric. Sew a straight seam around the outside of the piece of velcro. Finish the seam, and trim the thread.

Hook - and - Eye Closures

These can be used on any type of fabric, do not pull, are reasonably strong if sewn on securely, and don't add a lot of bulk. Hook and eye closures come in different styles, some with little loops, others with a flat bar, but the concept is the same. (Note: these would only be used on a neckline, such as the back of a collar)

Decide which side of the closure will be overlapping the other. On the under side, you will be stitching the "eye" parts of the closure.

The placement of the "eyes" is a matter of personal preference. Some people prefer to have the eye hanging over the edge, others like the edge of the loop to be touching the edge of the fabric. In the case of the "eyes" that are little flat bars, this doesn't really matter, as they cannot hang over the edge.

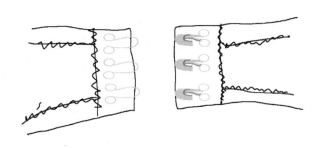

Stitch around the appropriate openings to secure the eyes to the fabric in the desired location. Makes sure to make many, many stitches for extra strength. Tie off and trim the thread after each eye.

On the underside of the edge that will be overlapping, attach the hooks so that the hooks are facing downward, and line up with the corresponding eyes. Again, make sure that you do this securely. Tie off and trim thread after each hook.

Swimsuit Hooks

These are one of my favourite closures, and they work well with illusion necklines. The only downside to swimsuit hooks are that they will snap under a lot of stress, and only work for thin closure areas (only an inch or less wide). You will need to add a 1 inch closure allowance to each side of the area to be closed.

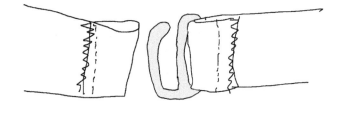

On one edge of the opening, fold over one inch of fabric to the wrong side, and stitch both 3/4 inch away from the fold, and ½ an inch away. If there are directions on your package, follow them if the width they specify is different (too big a loop, and the hook will just fall out)

On the other edge of the opening, pull the edge through the swimsuit hook so that the "hook" part of it will face up. Lay the edge of the fabric on the wrong side of that area, and stitch down, keeping the seam close to the swimsuit hook.

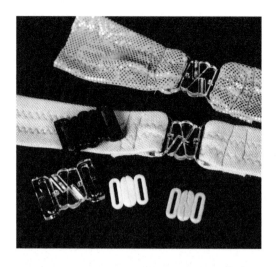

Butterfly Hooks.

Like swimsuit hooks, butterfly hooks only work on leotards where the closure area is narrow - 1.25" wide at the most.

Unlike swimsuit hooks, a butterfly hook is actually two pieces. They hook over each other to form an X (The "butterfly"), and when the X is flattened, the snap is secured in place.

These closures are nice to use - my favourite closure! - and very durable, but can be hard to find, depending on where you live. When in doubt, order from online!

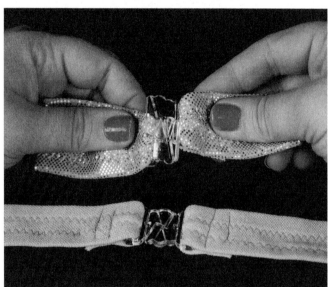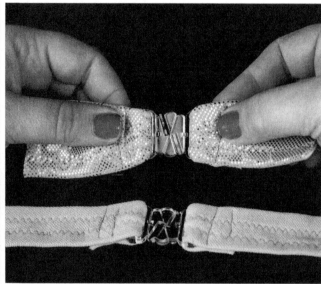

To install a butterfly closure:

1. Assemble the two pieces of fastener together. One side will usually have some sort of design (usually a flower), with the mechanics of the snap hidden behind it on the other side.

2. With the right sides of both the garment and the snap facing out, run one raw edge (where you want the snap) through one of the outer snap loops. The edge of your leotard may gather to fit in the loop, but that's alright.

3.   Pull a short length of the edge of your leotard through to the back, usually an inch or so. Remember, this will take away from the amount of fabric left to fit across the body, so be careful not to overdo it

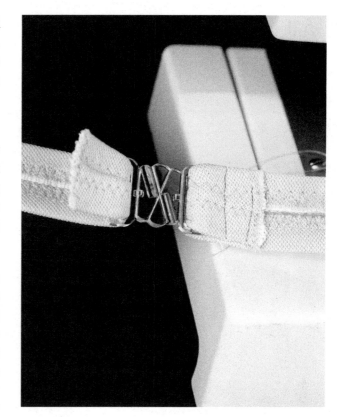

4.   On the wrong side of the leotard, you can sew the edge down as-is to reduce bulk, or fold it under for a more professional look. If sewing it down as-is, you should at least zig-zag the raw edge before installing the snap. (Pictured)

5.   Using a straight stitch, sew the loose end down to the wrong side of the leotard. Sewing close to the fastener will prevent it from wobbling around. If folding the raw edge under, be sure to stitch through all three layers - the outside of the leotard, the layer facing out on the wrong side, as well as the folded-under portion. If you don't catch the folded under layer in the seam, it will flap out.

6.   Repeat this with the other side of the leotard.

Now, that's the way you're supposed to do it... but there's an easy trick you can do to make this snap even more secure:

Sew it on BACKWARDS.

Yes! As the snap is most commonly used behind the neck, there is a chance that it will rest right over the prominent vertebra in the back of the neck... and crack itself open over it.

By sewing the closure on so that the "right side" (the decorative face of it) faces the inside of the leotard, you avoid this issue entirely!

In this picture, the wrong side of the leotard is facing up, as well as the "right" side of the snap. No worries - from more than a few inches away, you can't even see the difference!

Making Straps

Straps are basically covered lengths of elastic, used for all kinds of strappy backs. To make them:

1.   Determine how long you'll need the strap. I usually like to add up the lengths I'll need, and make one long strap, cutting off the lengths I need once it's done. Cut a piece of elastic that length - I tend to use the 3/8" wide elastic for most things, but have used a thinner elastic (1/4") for others. Play around with it to find what width you like!

2.   Cut a piece of fabric that is that length, by about 2" wide - assuming you're making straps that are about 3/8" wide.

 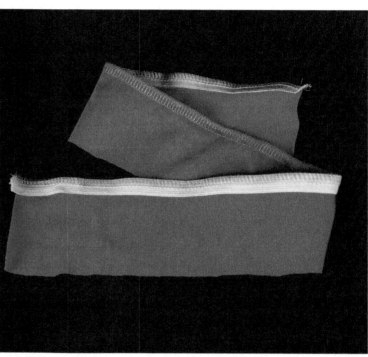

3.   Zig zag or serge the length of elastic along the length of wrong side of the fabric, keeping the edges together and stretching as you go.

4.   With the wrong side facing up, and the length of elastic on the right hand side, flip the elastic over to the left twice. Once will have the elastic facing down on the wrong side, the second time completely encloses it with the remaining fabric hanging out underneath it on the left side.

5.   Making sure that the fabric is tightly wound around the elastic (push it to the right, tightly), use a zig zag stitch to sew up the entire length, down the center of the elastic. Be very careful to keep the fabric tight around the elastic the whole way, or you'll have bulges of fabric when you're done.

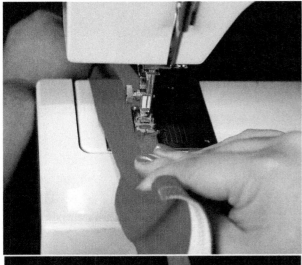
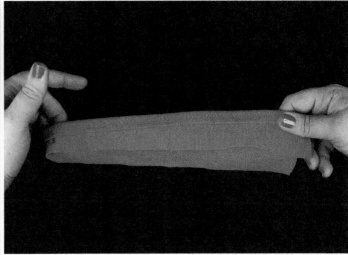

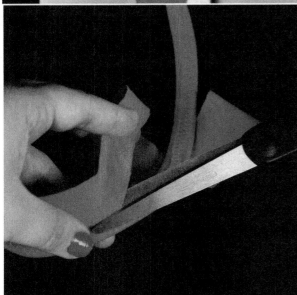

6.   Once you've sewn up the whole length, trim the excess fabric from the elastic, cutting as close as possible to the seam.

7.   Cut the long length down to whatever sizes you desire.

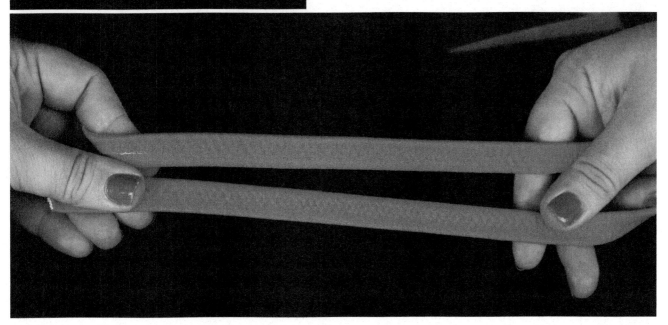

Hems

Hems are usually easier to do before attaching the skirt to the body, although if it is your first time using a certain pattern, or designing for a gymnast, you will probably want to do the hem after the leotard is constructed, in case you need to alter the length of it. There are a few styles of hems to consider

Cut hem -   Most spandex can be left unhemmed without worry of fraying, etc. This technique is one that you will use for petal skirts, or any skirt with a jagged, uneven hem. Make sure to use sharp scissors, and cut the hem in whatever shape you'd like - scalloped edge, triangle cuts, or random jagged. This is - by far - the most popular hem used in rhythmic gymnastics leotards. The cut edge is usually finished off with appliqued trim, hand painting, and / or crystals.

If you're doing a fairly consistent cut pattern - or want it symmetrical - it can help to fold the skirt in half and cut through two layers at once.

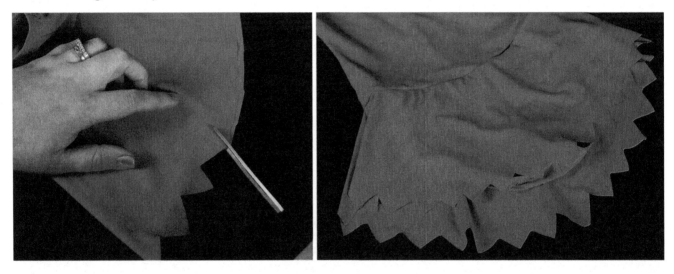

Flat zig zag hem-   Fold about 1/4" of the bottom edge of the skirt under to the wrong side. Using a medium stitch width, and a length of 8-12 stitches per inch, sew along the hem, being careful NOT to stretch the fabric as you go. A decorative stitch can be substituted for a zig zag stitch.

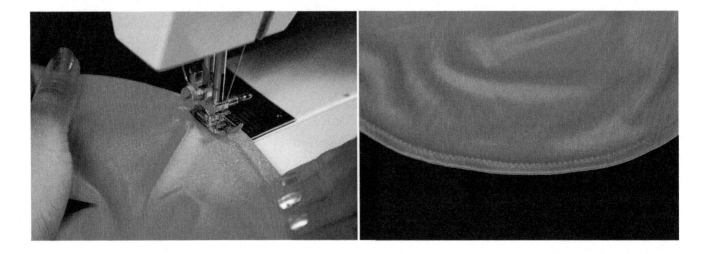

Lettuce edge hem -   Use a wide stitch width and a short stitch length for this hem. Stretch the fabric firmly as you zig zag over the raw edge. You may choose to let it roll slightly as you sew.

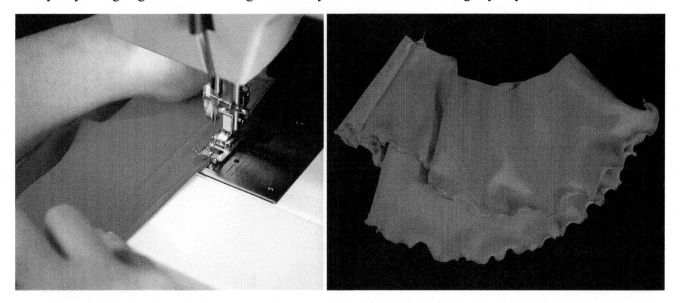

NB: When sewing a lettuce edging on stretch chiffon or a 2 way stretch lycra, keep in mind that only portions of your completed skirt will end up being ruffled. If you are doing multiple layers of 2 way stretch, (for instance, stretch chiffon) cut half of the layers with the stretch parallel to the grain line, and the other half with the stretch across the grain. Doing this will make sure that you do not have obvious flat sections to the hems of your skirt

Flat Serger -   Using a 3 or 4 thread setup, Set your cutting width to narrow, and use a shorter stitch length than normal. Serge around the edge, being careful to NOT stretch the fabric as you go.

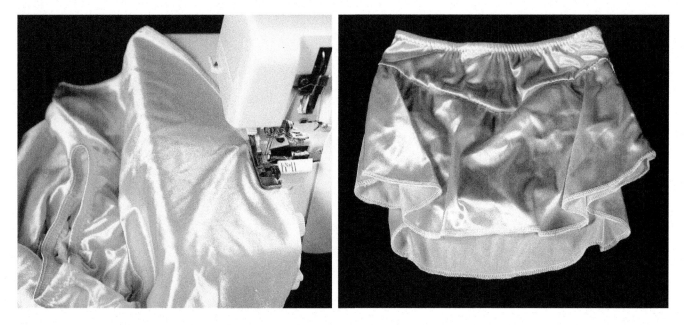

Lettuce Edge Serged Hem - Set the cutting width to narrow, following your machine's instruction manual for exact stitch settings. (Narrow hem, narrow edging, rolled edge hem, or etc) The stitch length should be short. Sew the hem as you would with the normal lettuce hem, stretching as you go.

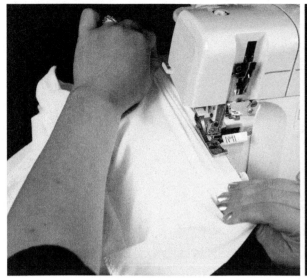
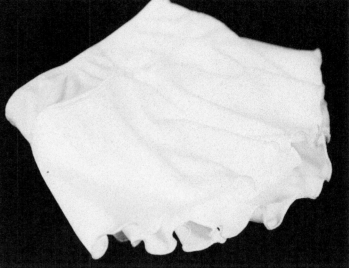

Note: If your fabric doesn't have a lot of stretch, if you don't stretch it well, and/or if your stitches aren't set to a narrow enough length, you won't get that much ruffle. Keep this in mind if you'd like a less curly, more wavy effect - pictured.

Fishing Line Hem

Fishing line hem follows the same basic premise of lettuce edge hemming, but with a twist. Like lettuce edge hem, the whole idea is to force the edge of the skirt stretched - with the very edge of the fabric stretched, and the fabric leading up to it NOT, the excess fabric will curl.

Rather than forcing the fabric to stretch with a lot of extra stitches, THIS hem stretches fine, sheer fabric over a length of fishing line. The clear fishing line supports the stretched fabric, and it curls over itself.

This is the sort of hem you'll see on a lot of ice dance dresses, as well as on things like children's pouffy pageant dresses. When it comes to rhythmic, this looks really nice as a layer under a cut hem spandex over skirt.

You can use a variety of sheer fabrics - chiffon, crepon, georgette, illusion, organdy, organza, voile ... but chiffon will be the most common you'll see.

As far as the fishing line goes, you'll have a bit of selection. Fishing line comes rated for strength - the higher the number, the more weight it can support. For the purposes of hemming, I recommend using a heavier line - 80-100 lb test, if possible. This is especially important if you use a heavier fabric. The flimsier the fabric, the less this is necessary.

As an example, I'm demonstrating this technique with chiffon, and 10 lb test line. As you can see, it works just fine - though a heavier weight line would provide even more structure. As with many things in this book, play with it and see what your preference is!

While you can do this with a serger, I prefer to use a regular sewing machine with a wide zig zag stitch - I just find it gives me more control, which is important for this kind of hem. Your mileage may vary, of course! Set your machine to a wide stitch with, and relatively short stitch length. Use a rolled edge hemmer foot if you'd like - I don't bother. Just a regular sewing foot and zig zag works just fine!

Generally speaking, you'll want to match your thread to your fabric as closely as possible - we did NOT, so that you can see the stitches better!

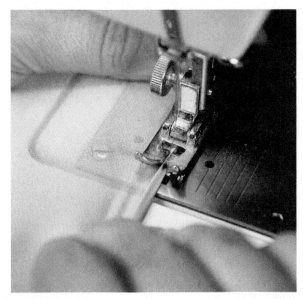

At the start of your hem, position your skirt with the wrong side of the skirt facing up. Hold the fishing line parallel to the edge of the skirt, and fold a very small amount of fabric over it. Fold fabric edge over once more, being careful to completely encase both the edge of the fabric and the fishing line. Make a few stitches, taking care to secure the edge of the fishing line in place.

Working a few inches at a time, continue to tightly encase the fishing line and raw edge of the fabric as you feed it into the machine. Be careful not to actually stitch through the fishing line, as it will kink. As you sew, easing the fabric, you'll also want to stretch the fabric as much as possible.

Now, as a note - I will use the line straight off the spool that it comes on, and like the wavy effect it produces. If you would like a TIGHTER effect, there's a fairly easy way to achieve that.

First, measure out the fishing line - you'll want a fair amount more than you need. Once you've cut the desired length, tape one end to a new "spool". It can be a small spool of thread, a thick dowel (say 1" in diameter), or any number of other things - improvise! Tightly wrap your length of fishing line around this new spool, securing the end with another small piece of tape.

Bring a pot of water to a boil, remove from heat. Submerge your new spool of fishing line in the hot water, allow to sit for about 5 minutes. Remove from water, set it on a towel, and allow it to cool completely - I like to leave it at least 2 hours.

When you unroll the length of fishing line, you'll find that you've reset the curl to it, and it's now got a much smaller radius to it.

Appliqued Hem

Applique is a great way to add some interest to a rhythmic leotard skirt. Once you have learned the basic techniques for applique work, you'll find that using it on a hem isn't really different from doing it on any other part of a leotard.

First, lay out all of your applique pieces on the front and back pieces of the skirt, being sure to plan for any overlap pieces.

Once everything is laid out, spray and affix your pieces, aside from those closest to the side seams - I like to leave 1-2" bare at every seam, to start. Once everything is affixed, sew the appliques on as usual. Once you've sewn all of the applique work on both the front and back pieces, place them with the right sides together and sew the side seams.

Flip the skirt right side out, opening to flatten one of the sides. Affix the overlap applique, stitch down. Repeat on the other side. (Pictured)

Once all of the design pieces are appliqued into place, flip skirt inside out. Using a sharp pair of scissors, very carefully trim, away the excess base skirt fabric, if so desired.

Note: If you plan to trim the excess fabric, I highly recommend using a spray other than Spray Mount for affixing your appliques. Spray mount will remain tacky after removing the fabric it has been stuck to. The other types will dry, and no longer feel sticky.

For this example, I trimmed away the base fabric that extended beyond the bottom edge of stitching only. For a lighter weight skirt, you can also trim away excess base layer fabric behind each piece of applique - in this example, that would be the pale blue fabric behind each flower and leaf.

See chapter on assembly for instructions on appliques that extend from the skirt onto the bodice (or vice versa!)

Leotard Assembly

Basic Leotard & Singlet Assembly

I think it's time for some "Order of Operations" instruction! Here is how you can take everything you've learned so far, and do a leotard from start to finish. For the sake of example, we'll start with a body suit shape, but with a lot of applique work. While shapes and design will differ, this technique is for mens' singlets as well.

1. Design your leotard, decide which size(s) you'll be using. Draft your base pattern, making adjustments for sizing / shape / leg height / etc as needed. Cut lining pieces from base pattern.

2. Use your sized base pattern to trace out a design pattern - the pattern that you will draw your applique designs on to.

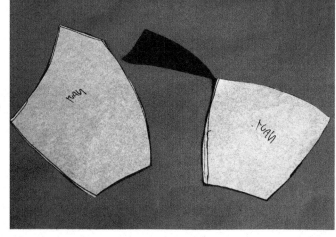

3. Use another piece of exam table paper to trace out each individual applique design. If mesh is involved, also trace the "suit" parts of your pattern.

4. Use your applique and suit design patterns to cut out all of the spandex pieces you will need. Cut mesh pieces needed.

5. Lay out lining pieces on work surface, if applicable. (If not, use your base of spandex, or mesh)

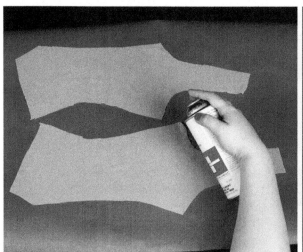
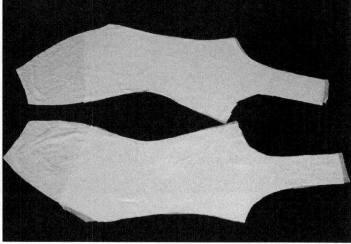

6   If using mesh, use Spray Mount to adhere it to the lining as needed.

7.   Without removing the backs from the pattern pieces yet, lay out your applique pieces to double check that everything fits where it should, and looks how you want it to.

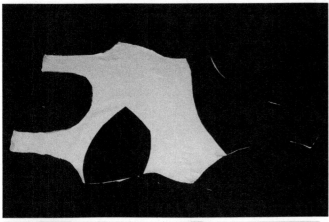

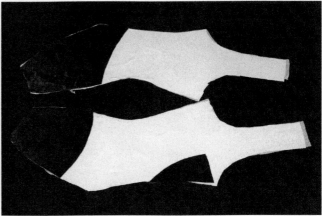

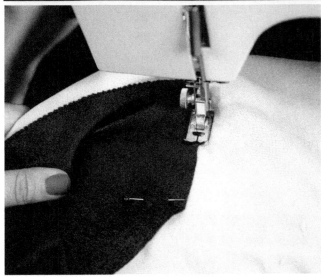

8.   If everything looks good, remove the pattern pieces from the base leotard pieces, and use Spray Mount to adhere base leotard pieces to the lining.

9.   If mesh is being used, pin these pieces down and sew them on using basic applique technique.

10.   Removing pattern pieces from the backs *as you go*, spray applique pieces for the first batch of applique. These will be the pieces that go underneath coming layers of applique.

Lay them out on the leotard, smooth out any wrinkles, and pin in place if mesh is involved.

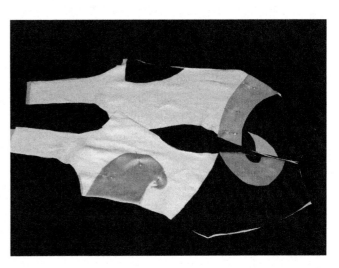

11. Sew the first layer of applique pieces into place, using zig zag stitch. Be sure to remember to stretch it all as you go!

12. Remove pattern backings from the next layer of applique pieces, if applicable. Spray the wrong sides of the pieces, lay them out, pin into place if necessary.

13. Finish sewing down all of your applique pieces on both the front and back of the leotard.

14. Sew the center back seam of the leotard.

15. If you need to do a line of darker stitching on a stretch of darker fabric (as with this example) beside the light serger seam, do so now.

16. Place the right sides of the front and back of the leotard together, sew shoulder, side, and crotch seams.

17. If you need to do any lines on stretches of darker fabric (as with this example) beside any of the light coloured shoulder, side, and crotch seams, do so now.

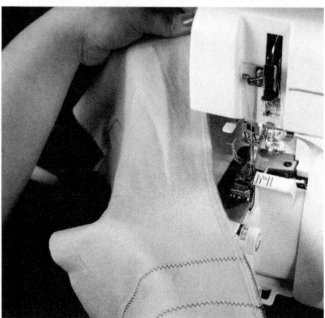

 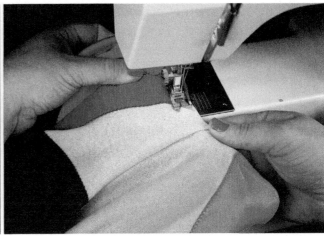

18. Apply elastic to leg, arm, and neck openings.

19. Flip elastic, finish off all openings with wide zig zag stitch. Change upper thread colour for different sections of elastic, if necessary.

20. Behold! You have a finished basic leotard, all ready to embellish, if you so choose!

This is the basic order of operations for anything you'll make, with some additions and subtractions, as necessary. If you're doing a sleeve, you'll need to apply it after you sew the shoulder seams, but before the side seams.

If you're putting a skirt in, you'll want to do everything below to the bodice and bottom , only sandwiching the skirt in when you have completed the individual parts. I'll get more into dress-specific assembly next.

Basic Skirted Leotard Assembly

Now that you have the basic overall order of operations, let's get a bit more specific - skirted leotards!

Note: There are two main ways of assembling a skirted leotard - the following instructions are for the method I prefer: Enclosing the skirt between separate panty and bodice pieces. See note following this section for details on the other method!

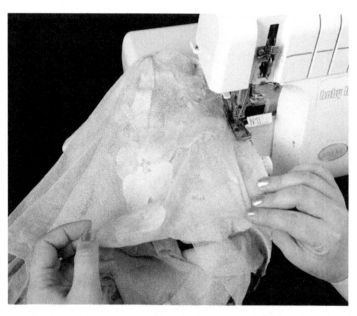

1. After designing your leotard & cutting out all of the pieces, do any colour blocking or applique work that you need to do, on any body piece that needs it. Be sure to keep appliques out of the seam allowances, if they're intended to overlap onto another piece when assembled.

2. Sew the center back seam, then sew the front bodice to the back bodice at the shoulder seams.

3. If you are putting in a sleeve, sew it on to the arm hole now.

4. Once the sleeves are sewn on, affix and sew any appliques that are meant to overlap from the bodice onto the sleeve, if applicable.

    In this case, the floral design extends from the front bodice, around the arm, and onto the back bodice piece, on only one of the sleeves. I left the seam allowance free of any applique, stitched the sleeve on, and appliqued a single flower to bridge the design between the two pieces.

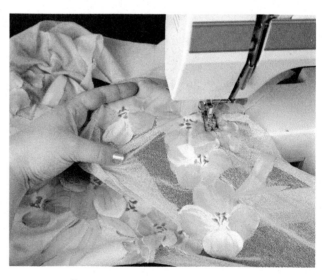

5. Sew the side seams. If sleeves are involved, you'll be sewing from the wrist all the way to the waist.

    In this example, one of the two sleeve side seams involved bridging the design from front to back, under the sleeve. In a case like this, you would sew just the side seam requiring the bridging. Once that seam is done, affix and applique the bridging design, before sewing the other side seam. Applique is MUCH easier to do on an open, flat bodice piece!

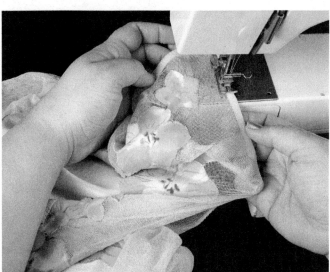

6. Turn bodice right side out, apply elastic to the neckline and/or back of the bodice. Flip and finish, applying any closures that are necessary.

7. Hem sleeve ends / cuffs. At this point, your bodice should be completely finished, aside from any final embellishments - crystals, sequins, etc.

8. Sew the skirt pieces together at the side seams. Right sides facing each other. If you are doing an applique hem, finish any bridging/overlap applique over the side seams before proceeding.

9. Construct the "panty" section. Sew the center back seam (right sides of fabric together), then sew the front and back pieces together, along the side and crotch seams- again, right sides facing each other. Turn panty right side out, apply elastic and finish off.

(Note: Step 10 (pictured at left) becomes optional when you become more confident in your sewing and handling - then, you just sandwich the bodice, panty, and skirt together and sew/serge through all 3 at once!)

10. Place the panty section inside the skirt, so that the front skirt lines up with the front of the panty, and the back with the back. Use a medium zig zag stitch to secure the skirt to the panty, right on the edge.

   Note: If you are doing an appliqued hem (as pictured), or have any appliques extending from the skirt onto the bodice or vice versa, pin them back, leaving about 1" of allowance for the seam

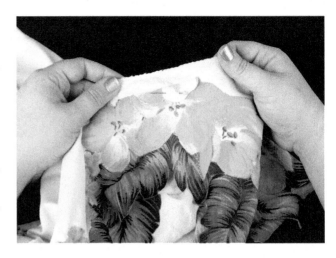

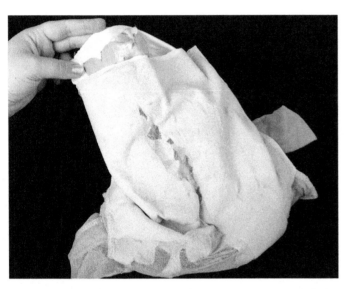

11. Turn the bodice inside out, and encase the skirt/panty section with it. Be sure that the front of the bodice is face down on the front of the skirt/panty, and the back on the back. Use a medium zig zag stitch to secure the bodice to the lower section, right on the edge. Finish with a serged edge or with a straight seam about 1/4" in from the zig zagged edge - stretching as you go.

12. Turn your dress right side out. Unless you haven't hemmed it yet, or have plans to embellish it, you're done!

13. If you have applique that extends from the bodice to the skirt, unpin and carefully affix it to the desired placement. You'll need to stitch it down in two parts - first the unstitched portion on the skirt, then the unstitched portion on the bodice. Be sure to pull any excess fabric out from under your stitching area - it is very easy to catch a wrinkle of panty section underneath when stitching the additional skirt applique, for instance!

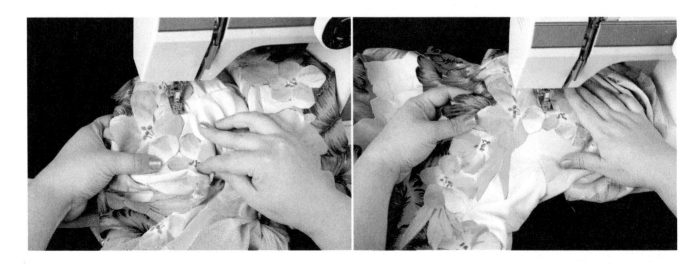

Ready to Embellish!

Now, as I'd mentioned... that's the first of two main techniques to assemble a skirted leotard. The second popular way is to sew a skirt onto a one piece bodysuit leotard, rather than have the bodice and panty in two separate pieces.

To assemble a leotard in this manner, mark your skirt placement line on the bodysuit with dressmaker chalk or a big, loose hand stitched line (to be removed later).

Once skirt placement line is marked, follow steps 1-8 of this past section. Rather than the piece you're working on be just the bodice, it will be a full bodysuit. Do NOT sew the crotch seam.

9.   Pin skirt to skirt placement line, wrong side of skirt over right side of the body. Take care to match up side seams and ensure that the front skirt is over the front leotard piece, and the back skirt is over the back of the leotard. Be sure not to pin the front and back pieces together!

10.   Going through the open bottom of the leotard, stitch the skirt to the body, stretching as you go. You can use either a straight seam, a small zig zag, or both - just be sure to stretch as you go, and stitch very close to the top edge of the skirt. (You don't want excess fabric to flap around, it will take away from the sleek appearance of the leotard!)

11.   Once the skirt is attached, flip the leotard inside out, sew the bottom/crotch seam.

12.   Apply elastic to the leg openings.

13.   Flip leotard right side out. If you have applique extending between the bodice and the skirt, follow step 13 from the main skirted leotard instructions. That's it! You're finished sewing your leotard, and ready to embellish it!

Tights & Shorts

Make any desired alterations to the pattern before cutting it out. Cut all pieces out of your desired fabric, with the greatest degree of stretch going around the leg. If using colour blocking, applique, or any other technique on the legs, do it before putting the tights together..

Keeping the good side of fabric to the inside, fold one of the leg pieces in half, and sew the inside leg seam, stretching as you go. Finish with a Serger or zig zag, and repeat for the other leg.

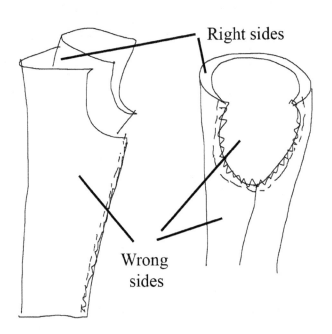

Turn one of the two leg pieces so that the right side of the leg is facing out. Put this leg inside the other so that the good sides touch, and the crotch lines up.

Sew the crotch seam, from one waistline to the other. Stretch this well as you go, and use a small straight stitch. You may want to sew a second seam over top of this, to reinforce the seam.(It IS a very high stress seam). Finish the edge with a Serger or zig zag.

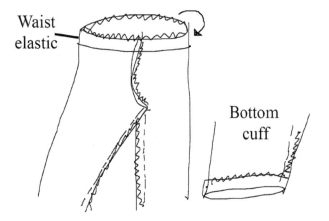

Apply elastic to the waist. It should be ½ an inch to an inch wide (check your pattern, make any necessary adjustments.

If your tights have a normal, straight edge to the foot / leg opening, fold the edge over to the inside and put a normal zig zag hem on it, stretching as you go. (Applying elastic is another option, for shorts. Be sure elastic is same size as leg opening!)

For Stirrup tights with no velcro:

After sewing the tights as described above, sew the
two stirrup pieces together, good sides facing each
other.

Hem both of the two foot holes, stretching as you go.

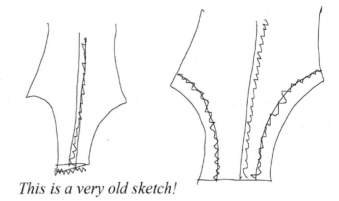

This is a very old sketch!

For Stirrup tights with velcro closure:

After sewing the tights as described above, hem both of the "U" shaped foot openings on the stirrups
WITHOUT first sewing together at the bottom.

Fold over the short, raw edge of the stirrups. Hem, and apply Velcro to the bottom edge of the stirrups

Unitards & Biketards

When it comes to unitards and biketards, there are many different pattern styles. Some patterns are basically
extended tights patterns, featuring only a seam up the middle front/back. Others are basically that, but also
involving side seams.

Other patterns have a basic tights bottom, but a separate bodice... or any of a number of variations on that
style. Still others have the front piece as one single piece, the back another single piece, NO seam up the
middle. These tend to be joined both at the sides, and with a single seam running up the inside of one leg
and down the other... with or without a gusset involved. Still others follow this basic concept in the front,
but with a seam up the back to allow for better fit.

Assembly is so dependant on the type of pattern used, that I'm only going to give some basic pointers here,
and advise you to follow the directions included with your particular pattern for assembly. The main things
to remember are the same things to keep in mind when it comes to basic or skirted leotard assembly:

- Have all of your colour blocking and/or applique work done before assembling the pieces together.

- If bridging applique across more than one main piece, follow the same directions provided in "Skirted
Leotard Assembly" instructions, as needed. Try not to involve any bridging on inner leg seams, as they will
be very difficult to stitch!

Applying a Sleeve

Generally speaking, you'll want to sew your sleeve on after you've sewn the shoulder seams, but before you sew the side seams of either the sleeves themselves, or the bodice they're being sewn onto. If your sleeve cap involves gathering, do that before applying the sleeve (See "Sleeves" in the Style Techniques chapter)

1.   Mark the mid-point on the shoulder curve of the sleeve, and pin this to the shoulder seam of the garment, with the right sides of the sleeve and garment facing each other.

2.   Hold one corner edge of the sleeve shoulder against the corresponding armpit of the bodice.

3.   Sew a straight seam along the arm hole, stretching both the sleeve and the bodice, easing the fabric as you go.

4.   When the seam reaches the mid point, grasp the other sleeve corner against the other armpit corner, and sew the rest of the way, stretching and easing the fabric as you go.

5.   Finish edge of seam with a zigzag (or serge) over the raw edges, securing them together.

Sometimes - rarely - you may want to insert the sleeve AFTER the sleeve seam is sewn. To do this:

1.   Sew and zig zag /serge the side and shoulder seams of the garment. Turn the garment inside out

2.   With the good side of the sleeve facing out, put the sleeve inside the garment so that the raw shoulder edge of the sleeve is lined up with the arm hole. Line up the side seam with the sleeve seam, and pin the midpoint of the sleeve shoulder to the garment shoulder seam. Any elastic gathering of the shoulder of the sleeve should be done before this. (See "Sleeves" in the Style Techniques chapter)

3.   Sew a straight seam around the edge of the arm hole, stretching both the garment and the sleeve as you sew. Finish the raw edge with a zig zag or Serger seam, also stretching as you sew.

Style Techniques

Backs and Necklines

Once you've gotten comfortable with your basic tank suit pattern, have some fun with it! Here's some information on alterations you can do to a base pattern, for different styles of neck / back. A lot of the techniques in this chapter rely on freehand, guesstimation, and instinct - so draw out your pattern as best you can, and be sure to make a practice leotard in case the first try needs tweaking!

Please note: Not all of these styles are "legal" for competition in all disciplines of gymnastics or related sports, but are included here for the sake of being comprehensive. Many work for practice leotards, or as necklines on related garments - sports bras, unitards, etc. Please refer to the rules of your particular sport for what is appropriate!

Crossover Back

This was my favourite type of back when I was skating. While it's not really used for competition leotards, it's great for practice leotards, skirted or not.

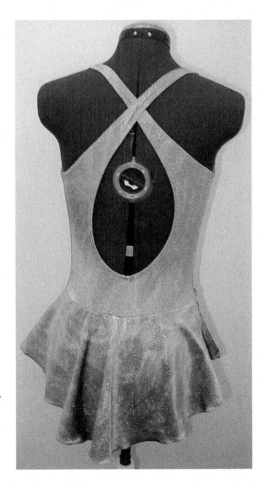

1. Trace the back portion of your pattern so that you have two copies. Tape them so that the necklines match up, side to side. You may have to overlap a portion of the upper back. Don't worry about being super accurate, the fabric will stretch.

2. Draw a straight line that goes from one armpit up to the inside of the opposite shoulder. From the point where your line meets up with the existing pattern piece, draw a short line that is perpendicular to the one you just made. It should be the same length as the top shoulder seam for the front piece of the leotard, usually about 2.5 - 3"

3. On the same pattern piece, mark a spot on the center of the lower back that is approximately where you would like the lower hole to end. Don't cut it TOO low, you don't want plumbers/gymnasts crack to happen!

4. Above that mark, mark a spot where you would like the lower edge of the crossovers to be.

    Draw a half-teardrop shape curve up from the bottom mark. See sketches. This style can be done really bare, really modest, or anywhere in between, depending on how you draw your teardrop!

5. Extend this teardrop shape up to the opposite shoulder, meeting up with the new shoulder seam you drew at the end of step 2.

6. Cut this pattern out of both the fabric and lining - you will need two opposite pieces of each. Hint: the lining doesn't need to go all the way up the strap. Cut it off at the point where it narrows out, to avoid some extra bulk!

7. Positioning the good sides together, sew the centre back seam from the teardrop down.

8. Lay the back part of the garment against the front, with the good sides facing. The back straps should cross over each other to lay against the opposite front shoulder. Sew and finish the side and shoulder seams, keeping the back crossed.

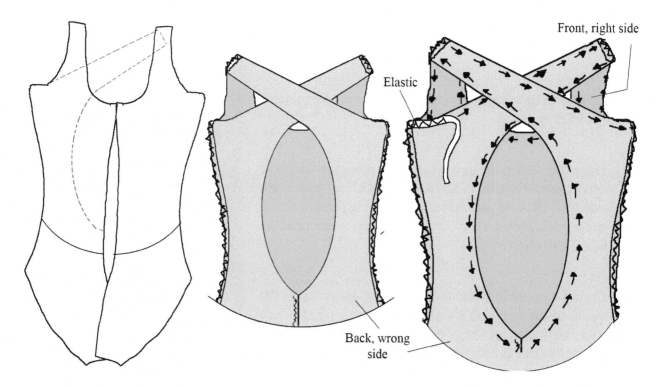

Elastic

Front, right side

Back, wrong side

9. Finishing this neckline will take one long piece of elastic. Starting from one armpit, attach the elastic all the way around, following the basic elastic application instructions. Stretch the elastic just slightly MORE than the fabric so that it gathers a bit. Flip the seam, finish it off with a zig zag, and there you go!

Scooped and Boat / Bateau Necklines

Scoop necklines are rounded - usually deeper than the standard neckline on a base pattern. You can do a scoop neckline in either the front, the back, or both.

Boat/bateau necklines are shallow, and elongated shoulder to shoulder - basically laying along the collarbone. To be a bateau neckline, this style needs to be done across the front. It can also be done in the back, or you can do a wide, scooped neckline in the back - your choice.

Scooped and Boat necklines are the easiest alterations you can do to a pattern. Basically, just draw the intended neckline on to the pattern. Cut out the fabric, and sew the garment, including any linings, colour blocking, etc. Apply elastic as usual.

For a boat neckline:

On the pattern (folded in half if necessary), mark a spot at the center edge (fold) of the bodice, just slightly down from where the neck begins. Boat necklines have a very shallow scoop to them.

Re-draw where the neckline meets the shoulder. This should be pretty wide out, almost to the sleeve.

Cut out and sew the complete garment.

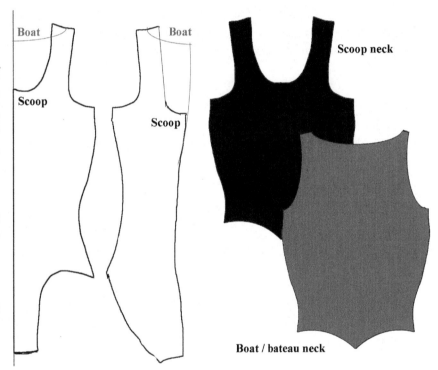

NB: As the boat neckline is so wide, a sportsbra lining is definitely recommended, to avoid bra straps from showing!

Hole Back

Hole backs can be done as small or as large as you want - a small keyhole, or almost backless! Hint: Use mesh and applique together with a hole back to create "fool the eye" looks, pictured to the right. This is an easy way to give some substance to designs using more delicate fabrics, etc.

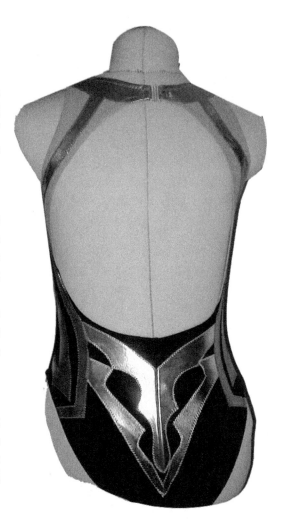

1. On the back pattern piece, draw your desired hole. Be sure to leave enough space (Usually over an inch and a half) between the neckline and the top of the hole to allow for elastic application. Plan ahead - know what size of clip you'll be using, and plan accordingly! (Height of the clip, plus 2x the width of elastic you'll be using.) Extend this opening about ½" - 1" past the original pattern piece, to allow for fussing with the snap later - you can always trim it back, if needed.

2. Apply elastic from one lower edge of the centre back neckline (closure area), around the hole, all the way to the other lower edge of the closure area. Apply elastic to the neckline, and the arm holes. Flip all elastic and finish off with zigzag.

3. Apply closure - ideally a butterfly snap - to both ends of the center back opening.

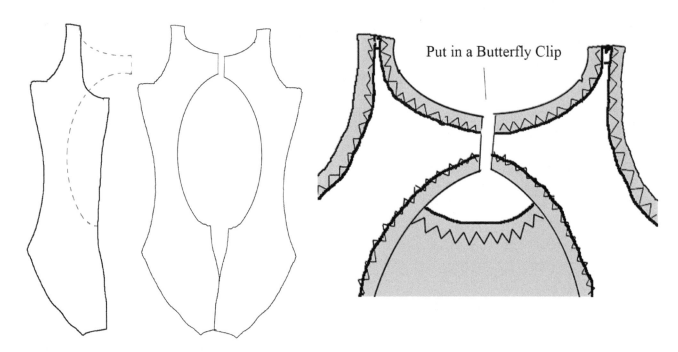

Put in a Butterfly Clip

Basic Halter

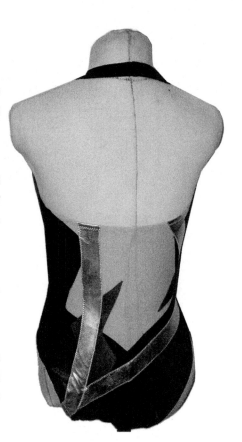

1. On the front leotard pattern piece, re-draw the neckline so that it curves/angles in slightly towards the neck, and extends beyond it by about 5".

2. At the end of the line you just draw, draw a short line that is perpendicular to it. It should be long enough to account for both the desired width of the finished halter strap, as well as 2x your elastic width.

3. Draw a line that curves up from the arm pit to meet up with the outer edge of the line you just drew (See sketch below)

4. On the back of the pattern, draw a line from the arm pit to the center back seam. This can be straight across or scooped downwards, depending on the style you would like to achieve. Play around with it.

5. Sew the side seams of the garment, with the good sides of the front and back facing each other. Apply elastic to both the front neckline and the back neckline, finish with zig zag.

6. Apply your desired form of closures to the back of the straps, trimming extra length from neck straps if necessary.

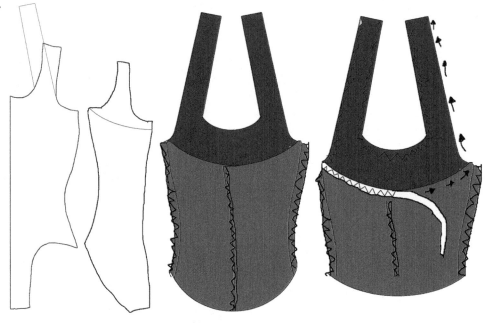

"Choker" Halter

For this style, be sure to use a pattern that has a high neckline - up to the collar bone - or alter your neckline accordingly.

1. Alter the front leotard pattern piece to reflect your desired neckline. Decide on the point that you would like the outer edge of the leotard to end at the neckline, and draw a new arm hole. This should curve from the arm pit up to the desired point.

2. Re draw the back line, as per the basic halter top instructions, and assemble the garment.

3. Apply elastic all the way around the back, from one edge of the front neck hole to the other. Do not apply elastic to the top front neckline area (where it lays across the collar bone). Finish off all elastic edges with a zig zag.

4. Cut a piece of leotard fabric that is long enough to go around the neck, plus 2". It should be wide enough to accommodate your desired width of choker collar, plus 2x the width of your elastic. Plan ahead - know what size of clip you'll be using, and plan accordingly!

5. Place this collar piece on the leotard, face down onto the right side of the front of the leotard. Match the center point of the collar piece with the center front of the leotard. Zig zag the top edge of the collar piece to the top edge of the leotard, stretching the collar piece slightly more than the leotard, and stretching both pieces together.

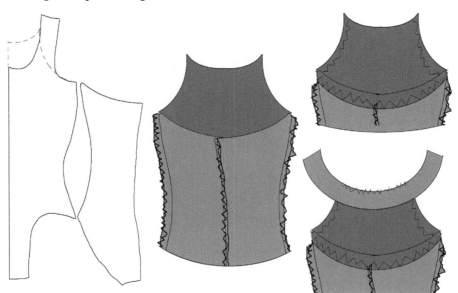

6. Apply elastic to both the long edges of the collar piece. On the section where the collar is attached to the leotard, be sure to sew through the leotard layers as well.

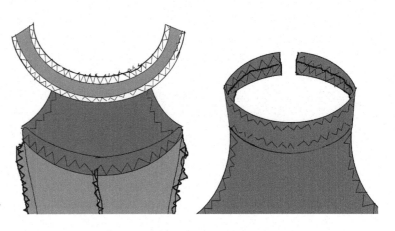

7. Flip and finish both lengths of elastic.

8. Apply your desired type of closure to the back edge. Fit leotard on gymnast, adjust length of collar if needed.

Basic Strappy Back

Straps are an easy way to achieve all kinds of different looks, with a little planning. Before you get into the crazy possibilities, let's look at a very basic application.

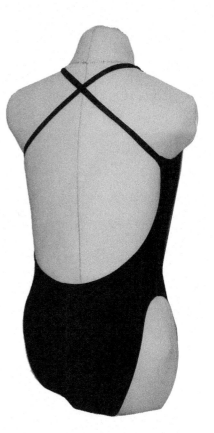

1. Alter the front of your garment pattern so that the shoulder tapers down to an appropriate width. To determine the width, add the width of your strap to 2x your elastic width. (A lot of the time, this will just be 3x the width of the elastic being used)

2. Following the basic directions for the crossover back, alter the back pattern for your leotard. Instead of the teardrop extending all the way up to the other side, however, this will end a few inches from where it extends out of the armpit - see sketch below. The line connecting the upper edge (extending from the armpit) and the "teardrop" line should measure the same as the measurement you came up with in step 1.

3. Cut front and back pattern pieces from both lining and outer fabric, sew center back, side, and crotch seams.

4. Cut two lengths of finished strapping. To measure for the length needed, lay the leotard out flat, and measure from the top edge of one front shoulder, across to the top back edge of the opposite side.

5. Sew one end of one strap down to a top shoulder edge, right sides together and centered. I like to use a straight stitch to get it in place, then finish the edge with a zig zag. There should be enough room on either side of the strap for applying elastic later. Repeat with the other strap, on the other front shoulder.

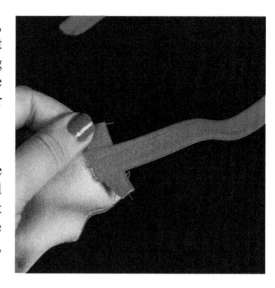

6. Sew the other end of one strap to the opposite side of the leotard, attaching to the shot edge you created at the end of step 2. Be sure to keep right sides together, and not have any twists in the strap. I find it easiest to have the leotard inside out, and just flip back one side of the back, laying the strap in a straight line to it before attaching. Repeat with the other side.

7. Apply elastic to the neck line, "teardrop", and what remains of the arm hole. You will start and end at a strap, each time. Fold the end of the shoulder / back piece under as you apply each piece - the seam you created to tack each piece in place should become the new edge.

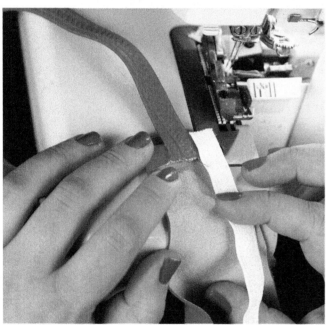
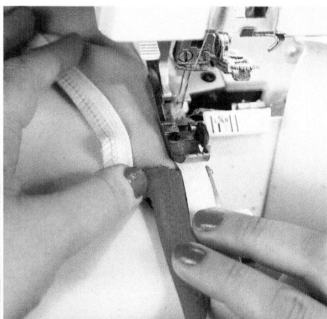

8. Finishing the elastic edge can be done as one big seam, stopping and turning at each strap end. Starting at one strap end, fold one side of elastic over the very end of the strap, and the end of elastic on the other side over that. Make sure that both sides of elastic are wrapped tightly up against the strap - this will give the cleanest appearance.

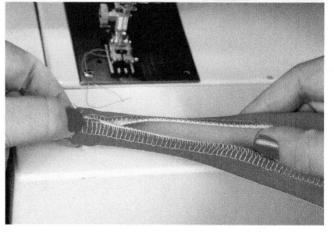

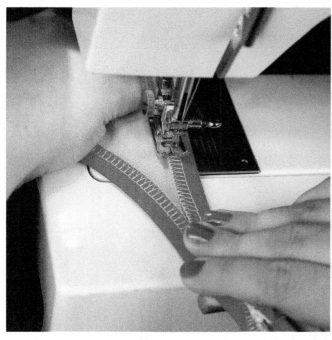 

9.   Start your zig zag stitch in the middle of one of these fold-overs, carefully sewing through all layers. Continue around your first stretch of elastic.

10   As you come up on another end of strap, stop sewing and fold everything over as in step 8. Sew up to the strap, continuing along the piece of elastic you are currently stitching down. When you get close to the strap, put your needle down, lift your presser foot, and turn the suit so that you'll be aimed to work down the next piece of elastic. Drop your presser foot, and continue along. Repeat until you come up to the strap you started on. Sew up to the strap, finish off your seam.

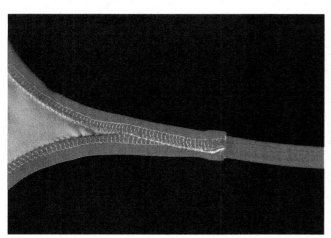 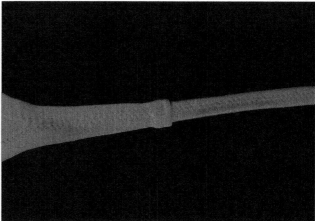

Multiple Crossover Straps

Now, there are many, many ways that you can do multiple strap backs. Here are some basic instructions to start with.

1. First, you will need to alter the leotard pattern for style. Before doing this, make sure that and required alterations for size have been done.

    The back portion of the leotard will be treated either as a halter back or the same as for the "Basic strappy" leotard (as pictured here)... and may be scooped as deeply as you like. As for the front leotard, you will want to trim some of the shoulder seam away, usually from the outside of the shoulder. To figure out how wide you will want the new shoulder to be, you will need to know how many straps you will be using per shoulder, how wide they are, and how wide your elastic is. Using:

    E = Elastic width

    X = Number of straps per shoulder

    S = Strap Width,

    .... your shoulder will be 2E + XS.

    For example, if the elastic width is 3/8", and you will have 3 straps at 3/8" each, your formula will be : 2 times 3/8" + 3 times 3/8" , or 5 x 3/8" = 15/8, or 1 7/8.

    Which means your shoulder width should be just a hair under 2 inches wide. For the sake of example, We will use these specifications to demonstrate.

2. Curve the outside edge of your new shoulder down towards the original arm pit, and adjust your neck line if you so desire. Assemble the leotard by sewing the side seams and centre back seam.

3. ON the right side of the fabric, attach 3 of your 6 (total) straps, to one shoulder, with their sides touching each other, and leaving an equal elastic allowance on either side of the group. Straight stitch them on, and finish the edge with a zig zag. Repeat with the other shoulder and remaining straps

4.   On one half of the back suit, mark off 3 evenly spaced locations for the straps to be attached to. There should be at least 2 inches in between the side seam and the strap closest to it (if using the halter back style), and at least 1.5 inches between the centre back seam and the strap closest to IT. Transfer these markings to the other half of the back, matching up the locations.

5.   Starting with the strap closest to the neckline on one side (we'll call this shoulder #1), without twisting the strap, pin it to the marking closest to the SIDE SEAM of the opposite side of the back. Make sure that all straps are pinned to the right side of the back suit as described under "basic strappy back".

6.   Repeat with the middle strap, pinning it to the middle spot marked on the opposite side of the back. Then, repeat with the strap closest to the arm hole on the front, pinning it to the spot closest to the center back seam on the opposite side of the leotard.

7.   Repeat steps 5 & 6 on the other side. Rather than laying it straight across, though, you want to weave them through the straps you already have pinned down, alternating as you go. If your first strap goes "over, under, over", the middle strap should go "under, over, under", and so on.

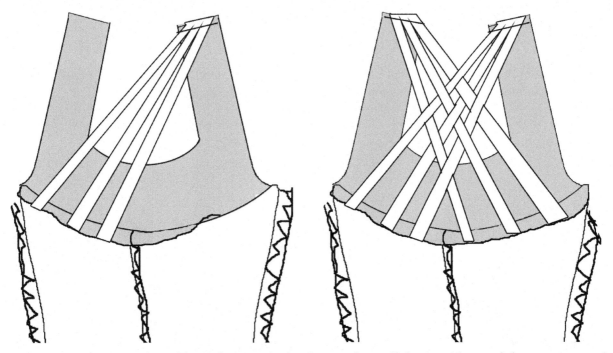

8.   Once all straps are pinned into place on the back, sew them all down with a straight seam, very close to the edge (as in step 3)

9.   Apply your elastic in 2 sections - one along the front neckline, and one long piece going from the outside of one of the front shoulders, all the way around the back, and ending at the straps on the other side of the front. Stretch elastic slightly, and then stretch elastic and leotard together as you sew it on.

When applying elastic to the back, be sure to stitch through both the leotard and the ends of the straps that are attached to it.

10.   Flip all elastic lengths and finish off with a zig zag. You will want to flip the shoulder seam allowances down so that they lay flat against the wrong side of the front leotard, folding the elastic down on top of it before stitching, as you did for "Basic Strappy Back".

Using these directions as a starting point, experiment! Some ideas:

-       Try one number of straps on one side (even just a single strap!), and another number of straps coming from the other side.

-       Rather than starting out with a halter style back, you can start out with the same back as the basic strappy back.

-       Experiment with how much of the back is open. You can do a very shallow opening (the back of the leotard cut straight across the shoulder blades), or very open (Back opening cut out almost to the side seams, and low on the back).

-       Use different colours. You can have all the straps on one side as one colour, and all the straps on the other side as a different colour... or have multiple colours across each side.

Need some visual ideas? Here are a couple different strappy backs I've done in the past:

T Shirt Collar

Depending on your desired look, a t shirt collar can be done to match, or contrast to, the rest of the bodice. In addition to being done with regular spandex, this style can be done with stretch mesh.

1. Determine the desired finished height of the collar. For this example, we'll say 1.5 inches. Add a seam allowance to that measurement (1/4 inch), and double it. (1.75 inches x 2 = 3.5 inches.)

2. Determine the length of collar needed. Measure the edge of the neckline - after sewing, and not taking the shoulder seam allowances into the measurement. , and subtract 1-2 inches. (1 for younger children, 2 for teens/adults). We will say that this measurement is 21 inches and for a child, so for example, the length needed is 20 inches.

3. Draw a rectangle that is - in this example - 20 inches by 3.5 inches. Cut this out of the desired fabric. Make sure that the greatest degree of stretch goes ACROSS the width of it. It should be stretchier from short end to short end than it is from long end to long end.

4. Sew the two short ends together, with the good sides facing. Fold this loop in half so that the two long edges are touching, with the good side facing out. Zig Zag along the long edges, securing them together. Make sure to stretch as you go.

5. Fold the collar in half, to create 4 equal sections - with the seam as one of the 4 folds. Mark the 3 other folds with a pin, or lightly with a pen.

6. Fold the garment neckline in half, with the center back seam as one of the two folds, and the center front as the other. Mark the center front point with a pin. Unfold, then hold the center front to the center back to determine the halfway point between the front and back, along the sides. These may or may not be on or near the shoulder seam, depending on how deep your front/back scoop necklines go. Mark these two points with a pin, thereby dividing your neckline into 4 equal parts.

7. Line the zig zagged edge up with the neckline of the bodice, folded edge pointing inward on the good side. Sew the edges together, stretching as you sew. Finish the edge with a zig zag or a serger seam, and flip the cuff out.

8. Pin the collar to the sewn garment, lining up the collar seam with the center back bodice seam, and the other 3 collar pins/marks to the corresponding pins on the bodice.

9. Sew along the neckline, stretching both the collar and the bodice edge as you go. You'll want to evenly stretch the collar slightly more than the bodice, to have the shorter collar ease to run evenly along the longer bodice edge.

10.   Finish edge off with a zig zag or serger.

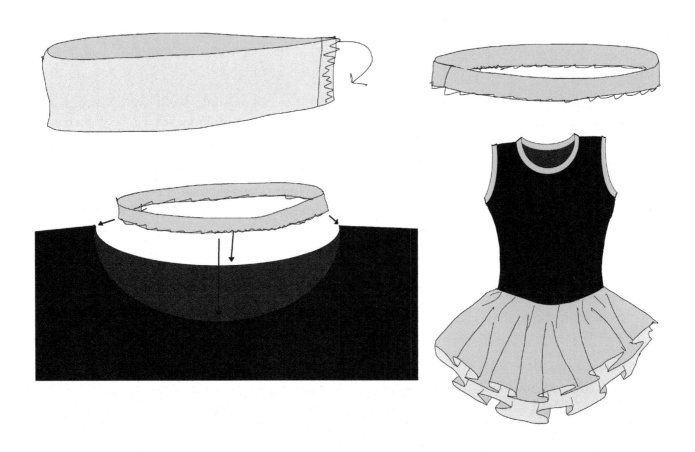

Note: *While pictured with a fairly shallow neckline, this technique can be used on deeper scoops as well. If going for a deeper scoop, subtract an additional inch when it comes to the length of the collar piece.*

Note 2:   *As pictured, this can also be used to finish off a sleeveless leotard or dress. Follow the same instructions, but make the collar about 2" shorter than the measurement of the arm hole. Play with it!*

Cutaway Neckline

The cutaway neckline is a cross between colour blocking, and applique. This is the method used to create sweetheart necklines, or accents with sheer mesh or Illusion.

1.   On the bodice pattern, draw your desired "fake" neckline. We will use a dropped sweetheart neckline as an example. Cut along this line, and keep both pieces of the pattern.

2.   Cut the bodice out of the desired main body fabric.

3.   Lay the smaller piece of pattern onto a piece of paper, and along the edge that was touching the main pattern, add 1 inch. Cut this out of sheer mesh or Illusion fabric. (Note: I freehanded, and wasn't the most precise with this in the example!)

4.   On the main part of the bodice, along the new "neckline", gently dab a thin line of glue stick to the wrong side of the fabric.

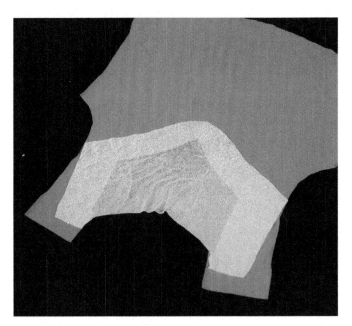

5.   With the good side of the bodice facing down, and the glue facing up, lay the piece of sheer fabric, good side facing down, on top of the glue. Make sure that there is 1 inch of sheer to the inside of the main bodice edge, the whole way around, and that the bodice is laying very flat, and is not distorted in shape. Press down and allow to fully dry, or it will muck up your sewing machine.

6.   With the good side of the garment facing up, and using a thread that matches the bodice of the fabric, zig zag around the bodice edge using the applique stitching technique.

7.   If using this method for a cutaway back, repeat these instructions for the back, then attach the front of the garment to the back of it.

8.   Sew the shoulder seam. If your sheer fabric extends to the shoulder make sure you sew the bodice part in the normal thread, and the illusion part of the shoulder seam in a lighter white or skin tone thread, if the illusion does NOT match the main bodice.

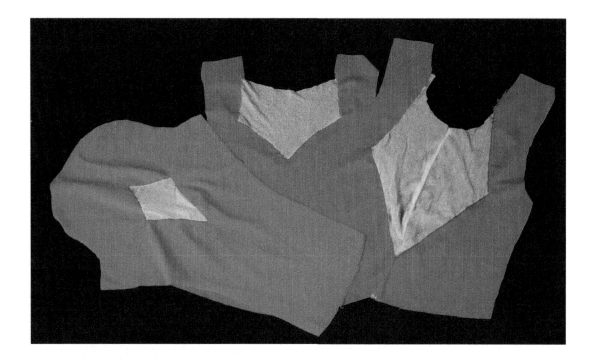

Cutaway neckline on front and back bodice, along with matching sleeve - reverse applique

Turtleneck Collar

The method for adding a turtleneck depends on if there is a hole in the back or not. If there is a hole, the turtleneck will be closed with either velcro, snaps, or hook and eye. If the back is full, a zipper will be applied. For a turtleneck collar, use the highest neckline of the pattern.

This collar can be done in mesh - usually skin toned - for a popular rhythmic leotard style. Once sewn in, it can be appliqued over as a bridging applique from the bodice, if so desired.

For a full back:

1.   Measure around the neck at the point where the intended upper edge of the turtleneck will be. Add ½ an inch. ("A").Determine the desired height of the collar. Add 1 inch. ("B")

2.   Draw a rectangle that is "A" long and "B" wide. Cut two of these rectangles out of the intended fabric. Make sure that the stretch goes across the rectangle ("A" should stretch more than "B")

3. Fold one of the rectangles in half, so that the short ends ("B") touch. Mark the halfway point (fold) on one of the long edges with a pin or lightly with a pen. On either side of the halfway point, mark the 1/4 points in the same way (divide each of the two new halves in half again). On the front of the bodice fabric, mark the centre point.

4. Pin the collar to the sewn garment, lining up the 1/4 way marks with the shoulder seams, the ½ way mark with the centre of the bodice, and the edges of the collar lined up with the centre back edges (zipper should not be installed yet). The good side of the collar should be facing the good side of the bodice.

5. Sew along the neckline, stretching as you go.

6. Install the invisible zipper

7. Sew a guide line on the second rectangle. It should be ½ an inch away from, and parallel to, one long edge. Stretch the fabric as you sew.

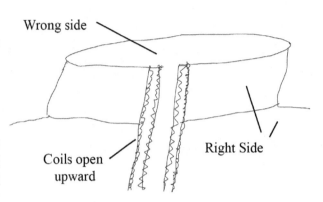

Wrong side

Right Side

Coils open upward

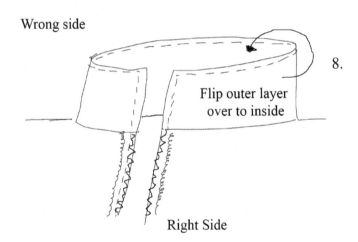

Wrong side

Flip outer layer over to inside

Right Side

8. Place the second rectangle over this collar. Line the edges up with the first (sewn) rectangle, with the good sides facing. The edge with NO guide line should be lined up with the raw edge of the first piece. Beginning from ½ inch away from the bottom edge (along the zipper), sew along the collar, sandwiching the zipper in. Stop ½ an inch away from the bottom edge of the second side.

9. Flip the second rectangle so that it is on the inside of the garment. Flip the raw edge underneath, so that your guide line is lined up with the neckline seam. Hand-stitch this guideline to the neckline seam, keeping the raw edge inside, and everything lined up smoothly.

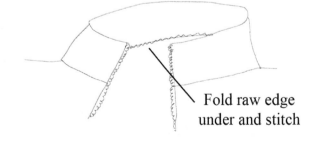

Fold raw edge under and stitch

Turtleneck for a back with a hole:

1.   Measure around the neck at the point where the intended upper edge of the turtleneck will be. Add ½ an inch if using hook and eye closures, 1 inch if using snaps, or 1.5 inches if using velcro to close the finished garment. ("A").Determine the desired height of the collar. Add 1 inch. ("B")

2.   Draw a rectangle that is "A" long and "B" wide. Cut two of these rectangles out of the intended fabric. Make sure that the stretch goes across the rectangle ("A" should stretch more than "B")

3.   Fold one of the rectangles in half, so that the short ends ("B") touch. Mark the halfway point (fold) on one of the long edges with a pin or lightly with a pen. On either side of the halfway point, mark the 1/4 points in the same way (divide each of the two new halves in half again). On the front of the bodice fabric, mark the center point.

4.   Pin the collar to the sewn garment, lining up the 1/4 way marks with the shoulder seams, the ½ way mark with the center of the bodice. The edges of the collar should be either .5, 1. Or 1.5 inches AWAY from the edge of the bodice, depending on your selected type on enclosure. The good side of the collar should be facing the good side of the bodice.

5.   Sew along the neckline, stretching as you go.

6.   Sew a guide line on the second rectangle. It should be ½ an inch away from, and parallel to, one long edge. Stretch the fabric as you sew.

7.   Place the second rectangle over this collar. Line the edges up with the first (sewn) rectangle, with the good sides facing. The edge with NO guide line should be lined up with the raw edge of the first piece. Beginning from where the closure allowance meets the bodice, sew all then way around the collar, to where the second closure allowance meets the bodice. Clip all corners.

8.   Flip the second rectangle so that it is on the inside of the garment. Poke out all of the corners. Flip the raw edge underneath, so that your guide line is lined up with the neckline seam. Hand-stitch this guideline to the neckline seam, keeping the raw edge inside, and everything lined up smoothly.

9.   Apply elastic to the "hole", attach your closures.

Skirts

Flat Skirts

In making your pattern for a flat skirt - the most popular style for rhythmic skirted leotards at the time of publication - you will be presented with several options, all of which will affect the final appearance of the skirt - amount of flare, length, how the flare is distributed, etc.

The first thing you will need to do is to make sure that the body suit portion of your pattern is suitable. After making any necessary alterations for size, adjust your waistline so that it is either straight across, or only slightly scooped downward. Deep "V" and basque type waistlines, for instance, are not suitable for the flat skirt style. Any sharp points or angles will not work.

Below, we have a few examples of waist lines that are suitable / not suitable for use with flat skirts

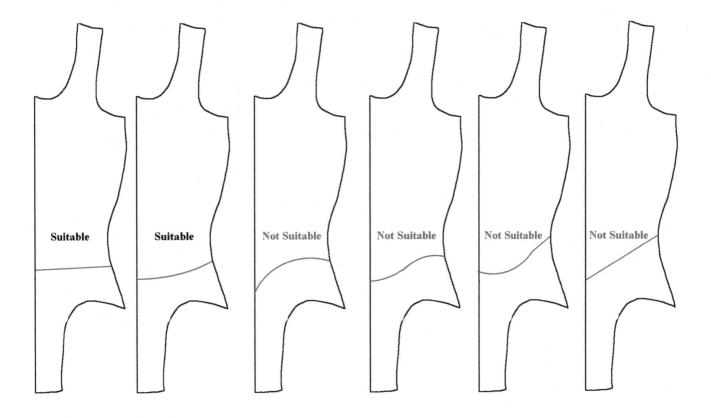

Suitable   Suitable   Not Suitable   Not Suitable   Not Suitable   Not Suitable

Now, there are a few measurements you will need to know:

1.) The intended centre front length

2.) The intended centre back length

3.) The intended side length

4.) The measurement of the skirt waist line, from the centre front/center back of the bodice pattern to the side seam.

Note: Flat skirts tend to look best when placed below the natural waist, sometimes as low as grazing the top of the hip bone. Know where you are placing the skirt before determining length. The centre back measurement is usually slightly longer than the centre front.

Decide on the style of the skirt. How much flare? Will the flare be evenly distributed around the whole skirt line,, or basically flat across the front and back of the garment, with the flare on the sides?

On to the drafting of the actual pattern....

Take a large sheet of medical examination paper, newspaper, or whatever else you have lying around, and lay it out on a flat surface.

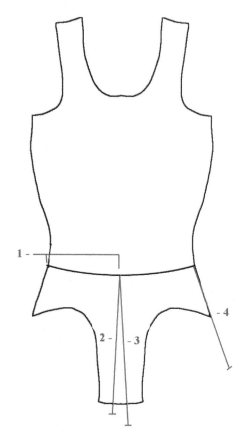

Draw a line which is perpendicular to one edge of the paper, and equal to measurement number 4.

Make another line at the end of the first, perpendicular to, and extending upwards from it. For the sake of example, we will use 1". This will be the side point of your skirt waist.

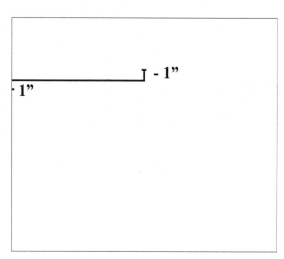

Below the original line along edge of the paper (which will be the centre front fold), make another point. For example, we will use 1" again. This will be the centre point of the waist line.

The lengths you use in the previous two steps will be a determining factor when it comes to flare. The closer they are to the original line, the flatter the skirt. The further away from the centre line, the more flare. 1" is a good starter measurement. With flat skirts, it's a good idea to make a practice skirts... or even a few of them.. to experiment with different measurements until you get the exact look you want. When you have the perfect pattern, make a copy of it on a heavy craft paper, like Bristol board, for a more durable, reusable pattern.

How you connect the points will affect the distribution of the flare. A smooth, even curve will result in even distribution of the flare. However, if the curve from the centre point upward is a long, shallow curve, and from the side point down is a short and deep curve, the result will be a skirt that is reasonably flat across the front and back, flared on the sides.

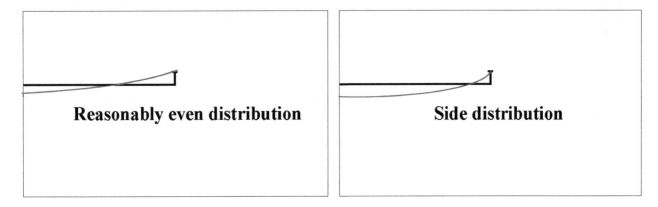

Reasonably even distribution   **Side distribution**

To look at this another way, where your waistline intersects the original line will give an indication of the flare distribution. A waistline which intersects the original line somewhat close to the middle will result in an even flare, the closer the intersection is to the side point, the more of the flare will be distributed on the side.

In the case of an evenly distributed curve, it can be easier to draw a straight line between the points, and curve it out in the middle.

Straight line
Curve it out

- **Center front**

Once you have settled on your waistline, mark a point below the new centre waist point (NOT the original centre line point), that is the length of your intended centre front.

When drawing the side seam, you must keep in mind that the seam must be no less than 90 degrees from the side curve of the waistline. Any smaller of an angle, and the skirt will not sit right on the side, as you will have more waistline than skirt which drapes from it. This results in a weird pucker.

90 degrees is good for a flatter skirt, if you would like more of a flare, use a larger angle. The length of the line which you angle out from the waist will be the length of your intended side seam. This angle must be at least 90 degrees

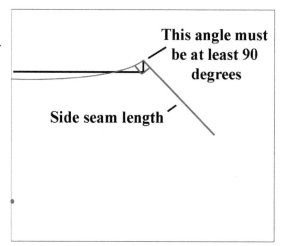

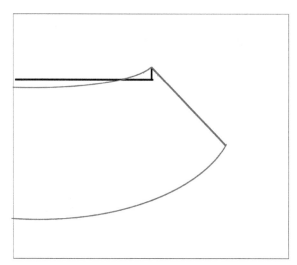

You will now need to connect the end of your side seam to the bottom centre point (hem).

An even bottom curve will be great with an even waist curve, however if you opted for a side distribution waist, you may want to telegraph that waist curve into a roughly equivalent bottom curve.

NB: If your centre front is longer than your side seam, then the skirt should get progressively, and evenly, shorter, going from the centre to the side.

To make the back skirt, either repeat the above steps, substituting the centre back measurement in, or cut out your front skirt pattern. Trace it on to a new piece of paper.

Along the centre edge, extend the line below the front hem, as long as you would like for the centre back . Re draw the hem curve on the new piece of paper. It should look something like this.

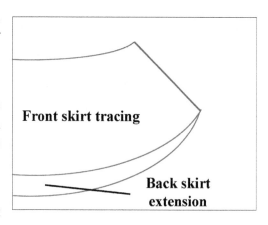

Cut both pieces from desired skirt fabric, placing the center front on a fold. Sew side seams, hem, and assemble as usual.

Multiple Layered Skirt

This can be done with or without cutaways and/or different length layers. This works better with a more full skirt, rather than a flat skirt style.

Make any necessary alterations to your pattern to suit the bottommost layer. Cut your bottom layer, front and back, out of the desired fabric. (If all of your layers are to be the same length, cut all skirt pieces with this pattern.)

If you are having layers which gradually get smaller, you can do one of two things. Either cut the desired amount off the pattern (say an inch) then cut the fabric, repeating for each subsequent shorter layer, or cut all pieces out, then trim the required amount off the layers which are to be shorter.

Sew each skirt back to the corresponding skirt front, and finish the edges as desired. (Flat or lettuce edge hem, serging, etc.)

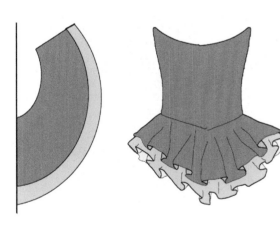

Lay your bottom skirt out flat, with the good side facing up. Stack all other layers on top of this, good sides facing up, ending with the top layer. Be sure that the front pieces, side seams, and back pieces all line up with the corresponding pieces below.

Zig zag around the waist edge of the skirts, securing them all together and stretching as you sew. Attach to garment as per usual.

Cutaways

Cutaways are another way to add interest to your skirt. These are done on multiple layered skirts, and work best if the under skirt is a different colour. To make cut aways:

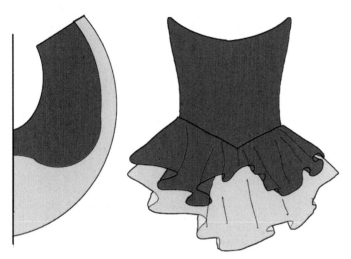

Decide on a shape and location for your cutaway. This could be a half circle cut out of the back of the skirt, for instance.

Another example would be to have an upper layer that tapers up on one side, revealing more of the underskirt on that side, than on the other.

For a shaped cut out, simply cut away as desired, and hem as per usual.

Slits

For a slit reveal on the side(s) of the skirt, hem both sides of both the front and back pieces of the top skirt layer - do NOT sew the side seams of this layer!

Hem the bottom edges of both front and back top layers, and assemble as described earlier, stacking layers and stitching together.

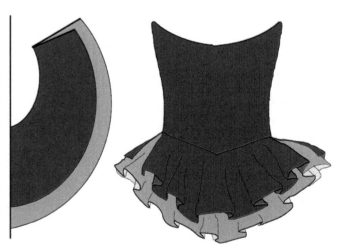

Alternatively:

On the pattern for your upper skirt piece, round the corner that joins the side seam to the lower edge of the skirt. Hem from the waist to the waist, on both pieces (front and back), and attach them separately to the lower skirt, without using a side seam for that upper layer.

"Tail" Skirt

An exaggerated style of skirt is very popular with ice dancers, but a more conservative version can be used for gymnastics - if you don't go overboard with the length. Because of the elongated, tapering shape, this skirt is very flattering, especially for people who are concerned about their butt. (I was!)

Lay your skirt back pattern on a larger piece of paper, with the centre back lined up against the edge of the paper. (Fold skirt pattern in half if necessary)

Determine how much longer than the actual pattern you would like the tail to be. While ice dancers can get away with almost any length, typically down to the backs of the knees... gymnasts should not go much beyond a few inches longer than the original pattern. Check your discipline's rules for skirt length!

Along the edge of the paper, continuing along the centre edge of the skirt pattern, mark a spot which is the desired length away from the bottom pattern edge.

Re-draw the bottom edge of the pattern onto the paper. For a fuller skirt, curve the new line out a bit. For a more elongated effect, be a bit more direct in drawing your new edge. See sketches. With the good sides together, sew and serge/zig zag the side seams. Hem and attach as per usual.

NB: For a full effect, curve the hem out starting close to the side seam. For an elongated effect, start re drawing your hem out at approximately the midway point on your existing hem.

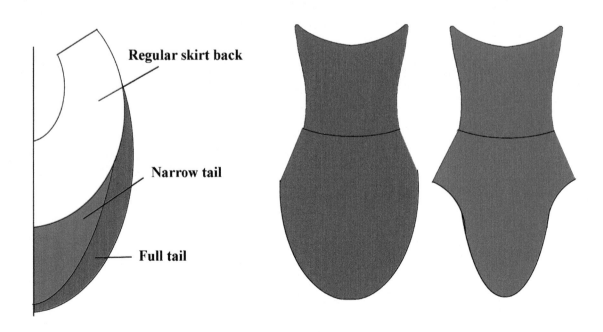

Regular skirt back

Narrow tail

Full tail

Handkerchief Skirt

This type of skirt works best with very lightweight fabrics such as illusion or stretch chiffon. It is made by attaching the corners of many squares of fabric directly to the panty portion of the garment, then continuing as a normal skirt.

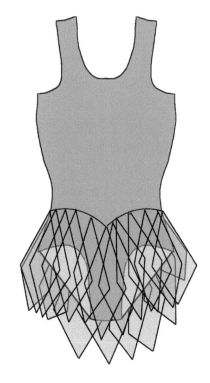

Determine how big your squares are going to have to be. The diagonal length of the square should be ½ an inch longer than the intended length of your skirt. If you are wanting for the back portions to be longer, cut two different sizes.

Cut a WHOLE BUNCH of squares out of the desired fabric. Don't worry if some squares are not absolutely perfect.

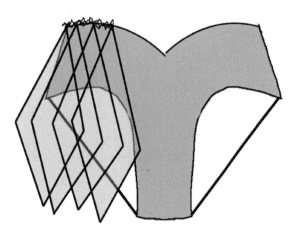

With the good side of the finished panty portion facing out, start at one side seam and start sewing the squares to the waist. Take one corner of a square and sew in on, and repeat as you zig zag along the waist. Add as many layers to this as you need, and stretch it as you go. You may want only a layer or two, especially if you are using a heavier fabric, or you may want many, many layers for a tu-tu like effect.

Once you have achieved the desired fullness, sew the bodice to this lower portion as usual. Be very careful that the squares stay put as you are sewing them, and that the un sewn edges do not get caught up in the waist seam.

Draped Skirts

This technique is not one that is used frequently, but it is a nice effect. This works best with multiple layered skirts made of lightweight fabrics (like stretch chiffon or illusion).

After assembling individual layers for the skirt, use a piece of clear swimsuit elastic that is shorter than the side seam of the uppermost layer, and stretch it to fit, sewing it right into the seam. This will gather the seam.

Assemble the layers as usual.

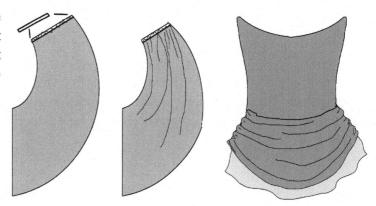

Petal Skirts

Another type of skirt which is not used too frequently is the petal skirt. This skirt is especially cute when used for very young gymnasts.

Cut "petals" out of your desired skirt fabric. These are usually peaked at one or both ends, curving out in the centre.

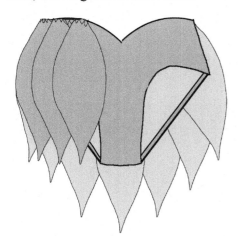

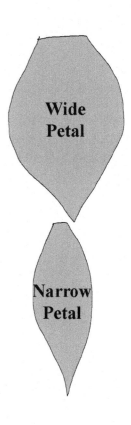

After assembling the panty, attach these petals to the waistline, right sides up. You may or may not want to overlap these slightly. There's no need for you to overlap and gather to the extent of the handkerchief skirt, in fact, that much layering would ruin the effect.

Assemble leotard as usual

One Final Note on Skirts

A tip for sewing the bottom to the top: If your waist has a "V" shape, rather than a rounded curve: Sew up to the point of the peak, stopping one cm away (½ an inch). Pivot the bodice piece slightly so that the un sewn half now lines up with the un sewn portion of panty part on the other side of the V. Be sure to keep the needle in the fabric as you do it, and that the bodice part lays flat, no puckers. Continue along the rest of the skirt waist.

Sleeves

You may find that you will need to add length to a sleeve in order or accommodate longer arms. For the average person, this can be done around the mid-forearm point. Follow the instructions for adding length, as described previously. Removing length (in a long sleeve) can be done the same as removing length from a torso.

If you are wanting a short sleeve, just mark where you would like the sleeve to end, and cut from there. It's that easy. In this section, I will discuss various other styles of sleeves, and how to make them.

Cap sleeves

Sewn-on Cap Sleeve

If you would like a separate sleeve piece on a cap sleeve, follow the instructions for making a short sleeve, but instead of cutting straight across the width of the sleeve, curve up from the under-arm seam to the center fold.

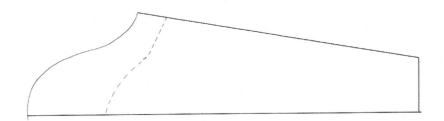

Built on Cap Sleeves

Cap sleeves can made by altering the bodice pattern, without the need for separate sleeve pieces.

On the bodice pattern, extend the shoulder seam out by about 2 inches (you can adjust this measurement as necessary, play around with it)

Draw a perpendicular line to the end point of the extension. This will be line "B". On line "B", mark a spot about an inch down from the shoulder seam.

From the neckline, draw a new shoulder seam in which curves down to the point which you marked on line "B"

From the point on line "B" to the bottom point of the original arm hole, you will need to draw another curve. This should be a shallow curve towards the top, getting deeper towards the arm pit.

Cut it out from desired fabric, sew side and shoulder seams. Finish the edge with a normal hem, or do a very thin contrasting cuff.

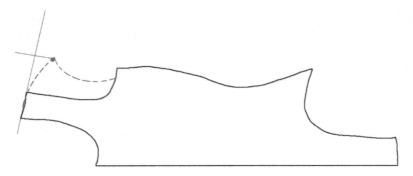

Leg of Mutton Sleeves

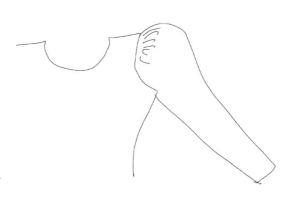

Leg of Mutton sleeves are fitted from the wrist to the elbow, flaring out for a more full upper arm, gathered in again at the shoulder.

Lie sleeve pattern on a large piece of paper so that the center line of it is against the edge of the paper (fold pattern in half if necessary)

Mark a point a few inches above the shoulder "seam", along the edge of the paper. The higher the mark, the bigger the puff at the top of the sleeve.

Mark a spot that is an inch or so about the elbow, along the CUT lengthwise edge of the sleeve (not the folded)

Extend the shoulder "seam" out a few inches from the original cut edge. The longer the extension, the fuller (widthwise) the puff.

Draw a line from the newly extended should seam down to the mark above the elbow.

Re-draw the top of the shoulder seam, from the new mark down to the extended shoulder mark. This will look like a bell. The wider the top of this bell is, the fuller the puff. If you have a longer, skinnier bell, the gathers will be right at the top of the finished sleeve, not evenly distributed. Play with it.

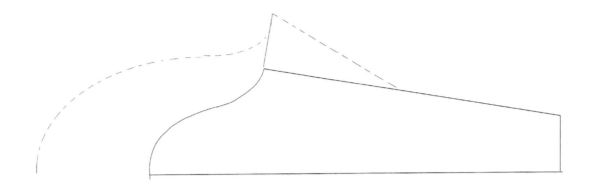

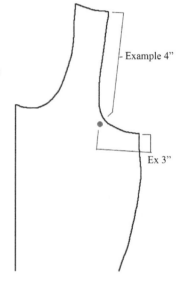

Determine how much of the sleeve you do NOT want gathered, from the armpit seam up. 3 inches is a good figure to start with, again, play with it.

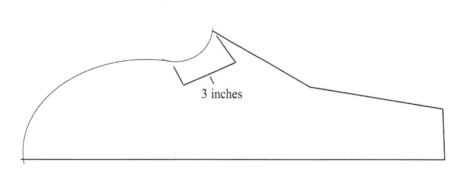

Mark 3 inches in from the side seam of the sleeve, following the curve of the pattern. On the main bodice, mark 3 inches in from the side as well. Note the measurement from this 3 inch mark to the actual shoulder. Double it, and cut 2 pieces of clear, swimsuit elastic this length*. For example, if the length is 4 inches, cut two 8 inch pieces of elastic. Mark the center of each of the two pieces of elastic, either with a marker or a pin.

Swimsuit elastic is ideal for this. If you can't find any, you can use a very narrow regular elastic

Secure one end of a piece of elastic to one of the 3 inch marks on the sleeve. Secure the halfway mark on the elastic to the halfway point on the "bell" part of the sleeve. Sew the elastic to the bell, stretching as you go to fit the elastic to the sleeve, thereby gathering the sleeve fullness. After reaching the halfway point, secure the other end of the elastic to the second 3 inch mark on the sleeve, and sew the elastic to the sleeve in the same way as the first half.

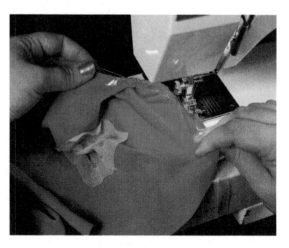

Because of the gathering, the edge of the sleeve top will now be the same size as the original, unedited sleeve pattern.

Sew the gathered sleeves to the bodice in the same manner as per regular sleeves.

Short, Pouffy Sleeves

Follow the directions as per the "Leg of Mutton" sleeves for the top of the pouf. .Determine the length that you would like the finished sleeve to be, from the armpit out.

On the pattern, mark the desired length.

Draw a line at this point, keeping it perpendicular to the center edge of the sleeve.

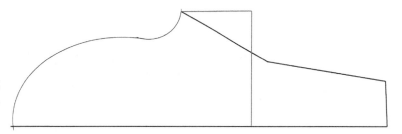

Complete the sleeve using the "Leg of Mutton" sleeve instructions.

Finish the raw edge of the sleeve with either a normal hem, or a binding.

These instructions will result in a sleeve that is not gathered around the lower edge. If you are wanting a sleeve that is gathered around the lower edge, follow these instructions:

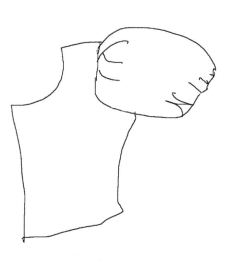

After making the necessary alterations to the top of the sleeve, and determining finished sleeve length, draw a new sleeve seam. To do this, draw a straight line extending down from the edge of the shoulder seam. This can go straight down (parallel to the center edge), or swing outwards for a fuller effect.

Measure arm around the area (say, biceps) where the desired sleeve length is. Cut a piece of elastic which is just slightly smaller than this measurement.

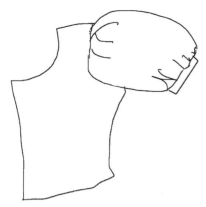

Apply the elastic to the bottom edge of the sleeve, finish off.

If you would like a cuff (Pictured to the left), only do the first step of the elastic application (do NOT fold it over and finish it off) - using clear swimsuit elastic - then apply the cuff following the instructions later in this chapter.

Double Layered Sleeves with Cut Outs and Ruffle

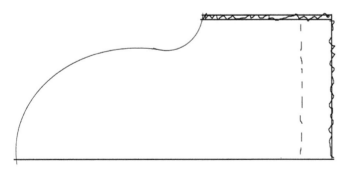

For a light and airy effect, this type of sleeve is best done with two layers of illusion, or stretch chiffon. For a different effect, Spandex, stretch velvet, or anything of the like may be used as well.

For each sleeve, cut two pieces (one over layer, one contrasting under layer) of the same pattern piece. Use the instructions for the short, pouffy sleeve with the gathered bottom.

When determining the desired sleeve length, be sure to add a few inches for lengthwise pouf, and another amount (measurement X) for the ruffle at the bottom. 2 inches is a good length for the ruffle, so we'll use that as the example "X" measurement.

Mark a line that is "X" measurement away from, and parallel to the bottom edge of the sleeve

On the over layer, make some long, lengthwise slashes in the fabric, stopping an inch or so BEFORE your "X" measurement line. If your over layer fabric may fray, treat the edges of the slashes with a fray stopping solution, or zigzag around them.

Sew the lengthwise seams in both layers, and finish the bottom edges with a normal hem finish, or a lettuce hem finish.

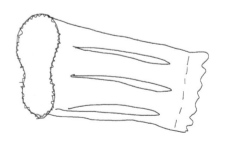

Put the under layer inside the over layer, with good sides of both facing out, and all edges and seams lined up.

Zig zag the shoulder seams of the two sleeve parts together.

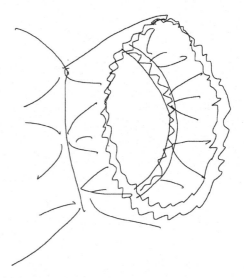

Pin the lower edges of the two sleeve parts together (only if you have to use pins, otherwise, just hold them together carefully), and sew a seam around the bottom edge which is "X" measurement away from, and parallel to the edge. You will now have your ruffle started.

Determine the length of elastic you will require. This will just slightly shorter than the measurement around that particular area of the arm.

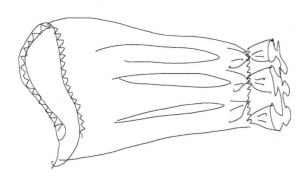

Attach the two edges of the elastic together, forming a loop. Sew the length of elastic around the inside of the sleeve, along the "X" line, using a zig zag stitch. Stretch the elastic as you go, in order to gather the ruffle.

Gather the top of the sleeve as per the instructions for the "Leg of Mutton" sleeve. Attach to the bodice as per the regular sleeve instructions.

"Morticia" Wrists

Have the rest of the sleeve pattern done, then:

With the sleeve pattern folded in half (if necessary), mark the halfway point on the available wrist. This will, divide the wrist into 4 equal parts.

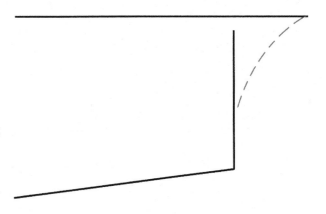

Continue the centre line of the sleeve out to a point that is as far away from the edge as you would like the centre point to be. Draw an arc from this new centre point, down to the halfway point that was marked on the edge of the sleeve.

This can be cut out and sewn as is, hemmed as usual (but following the curve of the peak), or you can sew an elastic loop to the peak before hemming.

For a faced wrist with elastic:

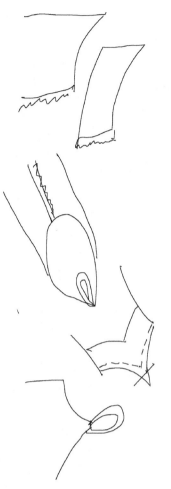

After cutting out the main sleeve (having followed the morticia wrist instructions above), cut another small piece of fabric which follows the edge of the wrist arc, but is only 2 inches wide.

Make a small loop of a thin elastic, and attach it to the GOOD side of the main sleeve.

Sew the side seams of the main sleeve, and its facing.

Line the facing up with the main sleeve, good sides facing each other, and the elastic loop sandwiched in between. Sew along the edge, stretching as you go.

Cut the small peak off the edge. Do NOT cut past the seam!!

Flip the facing so that it is on the inside of the main sleeve. Secure it to the inside of the main sleeve with a few stitches at the lengthwise seams, or sew another line around the bottom edge, on the good side.

Ruffled Bell sleeves

This type of sleeve works well with stretch chiffon, illusion, or other light weight fabrics. Decide if you would like a gathered top, or not. Based on your style preference, begin a pattern for either a "Leg of Mutton" sleeve, or a normal sleeve. Decide on a point for the bell to start, and draw a line across the pattern at that point, perpendicular to the center edge of the sleeve. Cut along this line.

Figure out what you would like the inner circumference of the circle to be. This will determine the amount of gathering around the arm, and the fullness. For no gather, your circumference will be the same measurement as the measurement of the arm at the point of the anticipated ruffle. For more gather, have a bigger circumference.

Draw a circle on a sheet of paper with your desired inner circumference. Measure the radius of this circle (draw a line splitting the circle in half, measure the line, and divide that by 2 .. we'll call this measurement "Y")

Around this original circle, draw another circle with the same center point. The radius of the new circle should equal "Y" + the desired length of the finished ruffle. Keep in mind that the garment needs to be functional, and the ruffle should not be long enough to get in the way of the gymnast! 4-5 inches is plenty!

Cut your circles out of the fabric. Finish the edges. If you are planning on having more than one layer to the ruffle, cut and finish all pieces, and stack them. Zig zig around the center of the circles to hold layers together.

If your sleeve is to be gathered, run an elastic around the center of the circles. This should be slightly shorter than the measurement around that point of the arm.

Put the good sides of the sleeve and ruffle together, and sew along the edge of the sleeve/ center of the circle. Stretch the fabrics as you go. Finish this off with a zig zag or serger finish.

 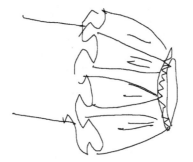 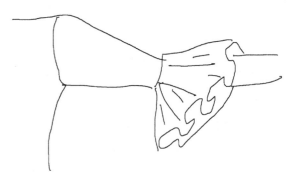

Retro Flared

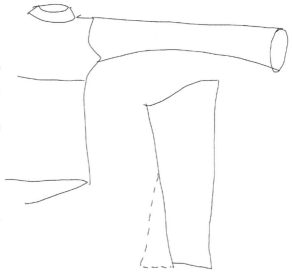

Start off with a basic fitted sleeve pattern, and do any alterations needed for length and fit. Trace this out on to a piece of paper. From the approximate location of the elbow, draw a new sleeve seam which flares out from the original sleeve.

Normal, fitted sleeve will taper in to the wrist. For this style, the new seam should be flared out slightly more than a straight, unfitted sleeve would be.

Assemble sleeve as usual.

Sleeve Cuffs

Depending on your desired look, the sleeve cuffs can be done to match, or contrast to, the rest of the sleeve/ bodice. Play with it.

Determine the desired finished length of the cuff (We'll say 2 inches). Add a seam allowance to that measurement (½ an inch), and double it. (2.5 inches x 2 = 5 inches.)

Determine the width of the cuff. Measure the edge of the sleeve (sleeve opening for a sleeveless garment - make a SMALL cuff edging), and subtract ½ an inch. We will say that this measurement is 8 inches.

Draw a rectangle that is 8 inches by 5 inches. Cut this out of the desired fabric. Make sure that the greatest degree of stretch goes ACROSS the width of it. It should be stretchier from short end to short end than it is from long end to long end.

Sew the two short ends together, with the good sides facing. Fold this loop in half so that the two long edges are touching, with the good side facing out. Zig Zag along the long edges, securing them together. Make sure to stretch as you go.

Line the side seam up with the side seam of the sleeve (or bodice), with the cuff facing the good side. Sew the edges together, stretching as you sew. Finish the edge with a zig zag or a serger seam, and flip the cuff out.

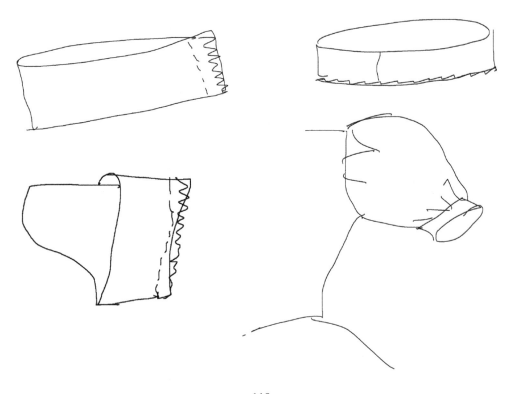

A Few Final Notes on Sleeves

1.   Sleeves can be lined, if desired. The easy way to do this is to just a fabric piece with the same pattern, out of lining, or even a contrasting fabric.

   Sew the side seams as necessary, and have the good sides of the outer sleeve and it's lining facing each other. Sew around the edge, and flip the lining so that it is inside the outer sleeve. Zig zag the upper edges (either the shoulder seam, or the elbow - bell) together. Attach to the bodice as normal.

2.   Keep in mind that many of these sleeve types can be combined with each other, or with other techniques such as colour blocking, beading, sequins or other embellishments. You may, for instance, want to use a Leg of Mutton sleeve, with skin tone "cut outs", and have beading or sequins around the cut out.

   In the case of colour blocking , applique, beading or other embellishment, make sure you do everything to the sleeve that you are planning to, BEFORE sewing it.

Embellishments

Before getting started with embellishing your leotard, you'll want to do a couple things - stretch the leotard, and decide what your embellishment plan is.

As far as stretching the leotard goes, there are several different approaches that you can take.

- If you are sewing for just your own gymnast, you can get a dressmakers' form and set it to your gymnast's measurements. Put the leotard on, and go!

- If you are sewing for just 1 (or a small handful) of gymnasts, you can build a bit of a stretching apparatus to use, out of PVC pipe and connectors. Search google for "how to make a synchro suit stretcher" - As of publication time, there is a good tutorial at www.frostyonline.com/nessa/Stretcher.aspx.

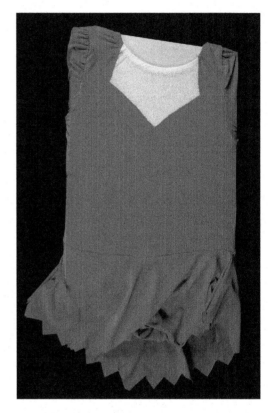

- If you're doing many leotards, or just can't be bothered to make a stretcher, you can use large, sturdy corrugated cardboard boxes. Get a few large ones - new moving boxes, for instance. Cut a piece of cardboard that is slightly longer than your gymnast, and half the width at each measurement point. If the gymnast has a 34" chest, the cardboard should be 17" across, etc.

- If all else fails, find a clean piece of something - even plywood - stretch the leotard over, and pin excess behind it. (Pictured)

When you know what you plan to do for embellishments, you may decide that you need to transfer a pattern onto the leotard as a guide. Tailors chalk or a disappearing pen can be used to draw your design onto the garment, if necessary - I prefer to just freehand it. Make sure you practice working with this method on a scrap piece of fabric first. Other things you can try are washable pens & transfer pencils. Always test methods on scrap fabric to ensure it will wash out, etc. Transfer pencil marks become permanent markings, so be careful!

Also, a word to the wise: No matter what method you use to sequin your leotard (or embellish in any other way, for that matter), you will lose some of it as time goes on. These leotards can end up taking a beating - it's always good to keep extras of any embellishment materials you use, for repairs after competitions.

Before starting on your embellishing, you need to have a plan for order of operations. This is especially important for rhythmic leotards, which tend to utilize multiple embellishment techniques. Here are some basic pointers, in order of priority.

- First of all, any applique work should be finished before starting on embellishments.

- If your embellishments are to include painting, that will be the first main embellishment to do. While you may end up deciding to do some minor touch ups after other embellishments are complete, you'll want the painting to provide the backdrop for everything else.

- After painting, do any foil embossing that you plan to do.

- After painting and foil embossing, do any glitter you plan to use... taking care to protect other areas from glitter! (More on that in the glitter section)

- Once all of those are completed and dry, finish with sequins and/or crystals.

Now, for the techniques...

Hand Painting

For any kind of spandex costuming, hand painting a garment is a great way to add a certain "something" to a leotard that you don't want beading or sequins on. The best example I have of this was one of my old competition outfits. It was a black karate - style dress, with a waistband accent with ties. Other then that, it was pretty plain, and sequins would NOT have been appropriate

I ended up painting the back. I used the bonsai-tree-against-the-sun idea off of the Karate Kid movie, and went to it. I stuck sequins into the glue for a little shimmer, without the "formal" appearance that sequins against the spandex alone would have produced. To this day, it's one of my favourite old competition outfits.

The hand painting on rhythmic gymnastics leotards goes way beyond anything you will see on pretty much any other kind of spandex costuming. Really, the rhythmic styles really put my bonsai tree to shame!

Now, painting is something that would take at least a whole book to teach, if going into detail. I can't teach you how to paint in this small section of a sewing book, but I can talk about the basics: materials, equipment, and some pointers.

First of all, materials: this would be your paint.

Personally, my favourite brand of fabric paint for use on spandex is Jones Tones. Once it dries, it actually stretches with the fabric. Jones Tones also comes in a glitter variety. It has a slightly less sparkly effect than actual sequins, but is a LOT more durable. It's a quick and easy way to spice up a boring fabric. As much as I love this paint, I should point out that it does have a bit more body to it than is ideal for very elaborate painting. It's not transparent at all!

For more elaborate painting - fading, gradient between colours, etc - there are a few options. Pebeo's "Setacolor" line of paints is very popular with rhythmic artists, as is the -Jacquard line of "Textile Fabric Paint". Whichever paint you decide to use, check the directions. Some will require a fabric medium be added, others will require heat setting. Jaquard has a product called "Airfix" that can be added to their paints to act in place of heat setting. I like this - it's always good to avoid ironing spandex if at all possible! (Also: never iron directly onto spandex! Be sure to have a thin dish towel in between the iron and your leotard!)

When it comes to equipment, you're mostly looking at brushes. Use good quality brushes in the styles and sizes you prefer. I don't really have a preference between natural or synthetic brushes, your mileage may vary.

Now, techniques:

- As mentioned at the beginning of this section, you'll want the leotard stretched before you start painting on it. As some paints can seep through fabric, it's always good to have a flat layer of waxed or parchment paper under the sections you'll be painting.

- Before you paint on your leotard, I highly advise doing a practice run of the full design on paper.

- Don't thin your paints with water - it can result in the paint seeping outside of your intended design space! (Of course, if you're looking for this effect, by all means - use water!). To achieve a paler version of your paint colour, mix in a little white paint.

- Paints will show up better when they are darker than the leotard colour. If you are planning an extensive, lightly/brightly painted leotard, I recommend just doing the whole leotard in white spandex and painting the whole thing!

- For the best definition, allow each colour to dry before painting adjoining areas. If you're looking for edges of colour to mix, allow the first colour to dry a little before adding the next colour.

- If you're layering colours, it's easiest to start with the lightest colours, and build up from there.

Ready? Just try to have some fun with it... and don't forget - what may look to be a glaring imperfection to you is likely not even visible from more than a yard away... and DEFINITELY not from the stands!

Once the base painting design is brushed on and dried, it can be fun to use other paints for accent. In the below example, I've brushed on some silver glitter paint, and then piped on some stretchy black Jones Tones paint - straight from the bottle - for some sharper definition lines / curls.

If your leotard doesn't call for a lot of intricate hand painting, don't forget - fabric paint can still be used straight out of the bottle for adding just a touch of definition as needed!

In the photo below, you can see that the floral fabric had very subtle lines of gold glitter printed right onto it. I used Jones Tones gold glitter stretch paint to highlight these lines, making the visible from a much further distance.

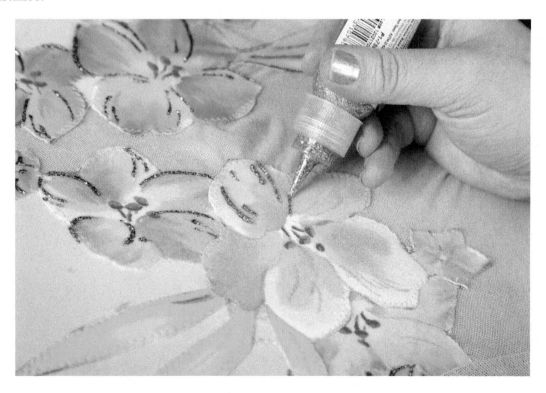

Foil Embossing

If I didn't sound like a total shill for Jones Tones by now, I'm sure that I will, after this section. I'm writing out of experience, and not being paid for this. I've just used their stuff for something like 15 years, and I've yet to find anything that compares. Tons of options, plus stretchability? Perfect!

Nowhere is this more true than with the Foil Embossing technique. It's a quick and easy way to come up with spectacular designs, and it's still fairly unheard of. I guarantee you, this will become a HOT technique! The effects produced by embossing foil onto a leotard are unique, interesting, and will have people marvelling at how you did it.

Oh, and it's spectacularly easy, too. Bonus!

Just use Jones Tones "Foil Glue" product to draw your designs onto a stretched leotard, and let it dry completely. (I like to let it dry overnight). This technique works both for "line" type designs, and for more solid pieces.

The next day, place some Jones Tones "Foil Paper" on it, with the design side facing up. Use one hand to hold the paper in place, and a finger from the other hand to firmly rub the paper onto the dried glue. You don't want the paper to move as you're doing this, or it could mar the design - think of how you would apply a temporary tattoo.

Once you think you've rubbed over the whole about, gently lift it off of your design. If you missed a spot, just reapply in that area.

124

Done... and it STRETCHES!

Yep. I love this stuff!

I'm a sucker for shine, it comes in a ton of colours...
and some are hologram! Have fun with it!

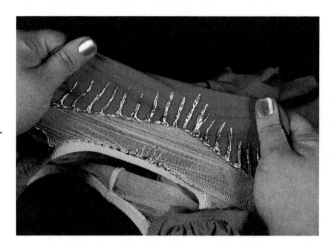

Here's a closer view:

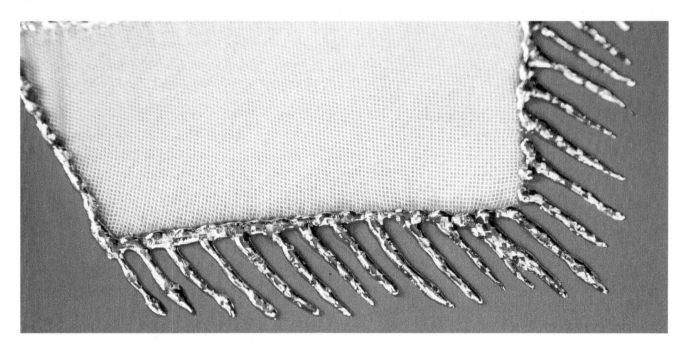

Glitter

Glitter can be used in conjunction with Jones Tones products to easily produce a sparkly effect that stretches.

Just stretch your leotard and apply Clear Plexi in whatever pattern you want. Sprinkle glitter of your choice over the area, and allow to dry completely before knocking the extra glitter off.

A few words of advice on glitter:

1. They call it "Craft Herpes" for a reason. Be very careful of your working space, when you're using glitter. You'll be finding it for months or YEARS after the fact.

2. If you are using glitter in conjunction with non-glittered hand painting, do the glitter first. Glitter will stick to Jones Tones stretchy paints long after it dries.

3. If you are applying glitter to a leotard that has mesh on it, block the mesh off with tape, spare fabric, or whatever else you have handy. The glitter will get in to the mesh and pretty much stay there. Similarly, if you have any exposed paint that is at all tacky, the glitter will stick to it as well. Best to just block off anything you don't want glittered!

Sequins

Sequins add sparkle and glitter to a garment, but can be rather fragile.. They are available in a wide range of shapes, sizes and colours from needlework shops, craft stores, and by mail order from specialist suppliers.

Sequins are usually stamped out of plastic and have a very shiny, metallic finish, but are also available in a transparent, clear, or iridescent "aurora borealis" finish.

Traditionally, beading and sequins were sewn on by hand, one by one. It was tedious work, but added a lot of shimmer and shine to finished leotards. Nowadays, most people use glue - which I'll address in a bit - but for the sake of completeness, let's look at how sequins and beads were traditionally done.

1. Use a good strong thread in the same colour as the fabric you are working on. Because the holes in beads are so tiny, you will require beading needles in order to do this. With a knot in the end of the thread, stick your needle in through the wrong side of the fabric, and out the good side.

2. Thread the needle through one sequin. This should be done through the flat side, coming out through the "cup". Thread the needle through a single seed bead, and back down through the sequin and fabric

3. On the wrong side of the fabric, secure the stitch with a few good knots, and trim the edges. Sew each sequin on individually, tying off the thread and trimming after each sequin. If you're coordinated enough to deal with extra threads, you can leave long loops between each sequin, on the back - cutting and typing in batches. Do 10 sequins, cut and tie all the loops, repeat.

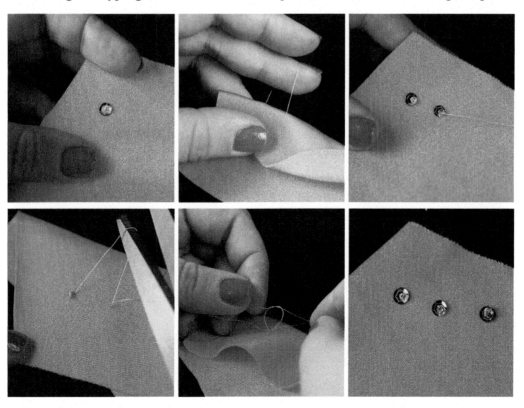

So... that's a pain, and also reduces the stretch in your leotard. The MUCH quicker and easier way is to glue the sequins on!

There are two main products that are used for gluing sequins on - Jones Tones' "Clear Plexi" - a stretchable glue - or E-6000 Multi purpose adhesive. Personally, I prefer the clear plexi: It's easier, less messy, and doesn't smell as awful.

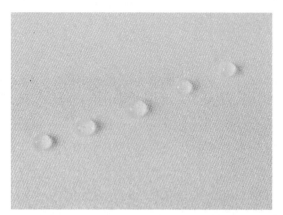

To glue sequins on, simply dot your leotard with adhesive, wherever you want the sequins to go. Carefully place a sequin - cup side up - on the glue and press down.

You'll want a "bead" of adhesive to come up through the middle of the center hole of the sequin, as this is what holds it on. Continue to apply sequins in sections, and allow to dry completely before taking it off the stretcher.

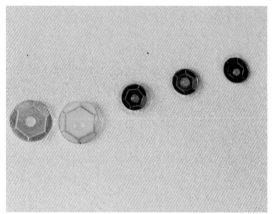

Crystals

Back in the day, crystals / rhinestones were either set on (with a pronged attachment), or sewn on (rhinestones that came with a sort of pronged "button" type apparatus on the back). Nowadays, crystals tend to be affixed either by "Hot Fix", or with glue.

Hot Fix Crystals

You can buy crystals - Swarovski or otherwise - with heat sensitive adhesive attached. While these can technically be ironed on with a regular clothing iron, I do NOT recommend that. If you'd like to use Hot Fix crystals, buy a Hot Fix applicator tool, which can be purchased for as little as $20 online. Follow the instructions included in your tool, to affix the stones to a stretched leotard.

Adhesives

While I prefer Jones Tones Clear Plexi for sequins, I slightly prefer the E-6000 adhesive for rhinestones. There are other adhesives that can work, just try them out first.

To glue crystals on, simply dot your leotard with adhesive, wherever you want the crystals to go. Carefully place a crystal on the glue and press down. You'll want a ring of adhesive to come up around the edge of the crystal, as this is what holds it on.

Continue to apply crystals in sections, and allow to dry completely before taking it off the stretcher.

You'll want to practice, to get a good feel for how big a dot of adhesive you want. The thing to keep in mind with the crystals is that they are attached to a mirrored backing, and the adhesives between the two parts is not all that strong - the clear part of the crystal can easily pop off, leaving a silver coloured, flat round piece.

By letting a ring of adhesive come up around the side a little, it adheres to the "crystal" part of the crystal, in addition to the mirrored backing. This makes for a much more secure adhesion.

Accessories

Scrunchies

Cut a length of fabric that is any desired length (the longer the fabric, the fuller the scrunchie, play with it).

To figure out the width, add 1 inch to double the desired width. If you want a 2 inch wide scrunchie, your width would be 5 inches.

Fold the rectangle so that the long sides are touching, and the good sides are facing each other. Sew along the long edge, stretching as you sew. You can use a serger (pictured), or a regular straight stitch/zig zag set of seams.

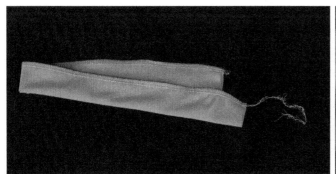 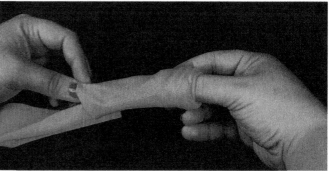

Turn the scrunchie so that the right side is facing out. Run an elastic through the scrunchie, bunching the fabric as you go. Tie the two ends of elastic together a couple times so that it forms a loop of the desired length.

 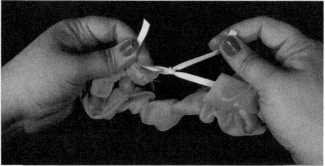

Straighten out the fabric so that the seam line forms a continuous path around the elastic - I like to position it facing out. With one edge of fabric overlapping the other, either sew through all layers with your machine or hand sew around the opening.

Grip Bags

Grip bags are quick and easy to make, and a fun way to personalize a gymnast's equipment. You can use pretty much any kind of fabric for them, from fun printed quit fabric, to glitzy metallic spandex.

Sizing of grip bags is completely up to you... theyounger gymnasts will usually use smaller bags, while older girls tend to have more stuff to carry - butt glue, tape, etc in addition to their handgrips. As an example, this grip bag demonstration used two pieces of fabric that were cut to roughly 8 x 11 inches.

To begin, serge or zig zag around each edge of both pieces of your cut fabric. Place the piece with right sides facing each other. If you'd like to, pin the two pieces together.

Starting on what will be one of the sides, start a straight stitch seam about 2" below what will be the top edge of the bag. Stitch down the side to the bottom, pivot, sew across the bottom. Pivot, sew up the other side, ending 2" from the top.

Open your bag a little, to be able to flatten one of the side seams. Press open the seam near the top, using either your fingers or an iron. (I'm too lazy to bother with an iron!).

Starting at one top edge, stitch the flap of the seam down, ending just below where the original seam started. Pivot, sewing a short seam across the bottom of this v shaped opening, and ending almost at the serged edge of the other side. Pivot, and sew the other side flap down, ending at the top edge.

Fold the top edge of the bag over 1", with the right side facing out. Press it down, again either with fingers or an iron. Repeat on the other side.

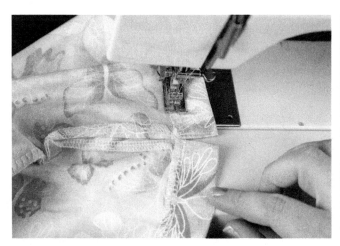 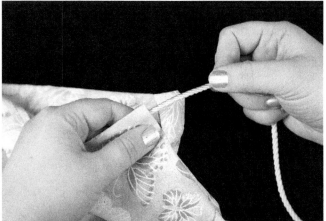

Sew a straight seam along the serged (formerly!) top edge of the bag, the whole way around. Stitch over the initial few stitches when you reach the starting point, then stitch back and forth a couple of times for extra security.

Turn bag right side out.

Run a cord through the top channel of the bag. Tie the two ends of cord together a couple times so that it forms a loop of the desired length. Trim very ends of cord, if necessary.

Proper Care of Leotards

Practice Leotards:

-   To wash untrimmed practice leotards, turn leotard inside out and machine wash on a gentle cycle, with a mild detergent. Tumble dry on low heat.

-   White or pale coloured leotards have a tendency to stain in certain areas - neckline, sleeve edges, collars, underarm, and crotch. To prevent this staining, you may want to treat these areas (not the whole leotard) with ScotchGuard treatment, following manufacturer's directions.

(For leotards with any sort of sequin or rhinestone trim, treat it as a competition leotard)

Competition Leotards:

-   Immediately after use, spritz sweat soiled areas with vodka. This helps sanitize and prevent bacterial growth / smell, without the need for actually washing it.

-   Small areas may be spot washed as necessary. Gently rub affected area with warm water and a mild detergent, rinse thoroughly and allow to air dry.

-   If you absolutely must wash your entire competition leotard, hand wash the leotard in cool water with a small amount of a very gentle, Spandex-specific wash. (Available in lingerie sections of department stores). Always wash by hand, NEVER in a washing machine.

-   Never ring your leotard out! After rinsing/washing, gently roll leotard in an absorbent towel for a few minutes before allowing to air dry. Never use heat or direct sunlight to dry your leotards, and never put them away wet.

-   Never hang up a wet leotard. If your leotard is very heavy from a lot of rhinestones, it may be best to not hang it, even when dry.

-   Examine your leotard after it dries, make any repairs to lost embellishments if necessary. If storing / travelling with multiple competition leotards, find some acid free tissue paper to place between them.

Resources

This list is for informational purposes only, and does not necessarily constitute an endorsement of any of these companies. We do not receive payment of any kind by these companies for being listed here. It is the readers' responsibility to properly vet any companies they choose to do business with; we are not responsible for any disputes that may arise.

Books

Spandex Simplified   www.spandexsimplified.com

Patterns

Kwik-Sew Pattern Co.   www.kwiksew.mccall.com
Sew Sassy   www.sewsassy.com
Stretch & Sew   www.stretch-and-sew.com
Jalie   www.jalie.com

Fabrics

Spandex House   www.spandexhouse.com
Spandex World   www.spandexworld.com
Stretch Text   www.stretchtextfabrics.com

Embellishments

Jones Tones   www.jonestones.com
Sparkle Haven   www.sparklehaven.com

Notes

Notes

Notes

Notes

The Spirited Baker

Intoxicating Desserts & Potent Potables

Combining liqueurs with more traditional baking ingredients can yield spectacular results. Try Mango Mojito Upside Down Cake, Candy Apple Flan, Jalapeno Beer Peanut Brittle, Lynchburg Lemonade Cupcakes, Pina Colada Rum Cake, Strawberry Daiquiri Chiffon Pie, and so much more.

To further add to your creative possibilities, the first chapter teaches how to infuse spirits to make both basic and cream liqueurs, as well as home made flavor extracts! This book contains over 160 easy to make recipes, with variation suggestions to help create hundreds more!

Sweet Corn Spectacular

The height of summer brings with it the bounty of fresh sweet corn. Grilled or boiled, slathered in butter and sprinkled with salt, corn on the cob is a mainstay of cook-out menus. But this "vegetable" can grace your plate in so many other ways. In fact, author and baker Marie Porter once devised an entire day's worth of corn-based dishes to celebrate her "corn freak"husband's birthday.

Sweet Corn Spectacular displays Porter's creative and flavor-filled approach to this North American original, inspiring year-round use of this versatile ingredient and tasty experimenting in your own kitchen. As Porter reminds home cooks, the possibilities are endless!

Evil Cake Overlord

Ridiculously Delicious Cakes

Celebration Generation has been known for our "ridiculously delicious" moist cakes and tasty, unique flavors since the genesis of our custom cake business. Now, you can have recipes for all of the amazing flavors on our former custom cake menu, as well as many more!

Once you have baked your moist work of gastronomic art, fill and frost your cake with any number of tasty possibilities. Milk chocolate cardamom pear, mango mojito.. even our famous Chai cake - the flavor that got us into "Every Day with Rachel Ray" magazine! Feeling creative? Use our easy to follow recipe to make our yummy fondant. Forget everything you've heard about fondant - ours is made from marshmallows and powdered sugar, and is essentially candy - you can even flavor it to bring a whole new level of "yum!" to every cake you make!

For wholesale inquiries or to purchase directly, visit

www.celebrationgeneration.com

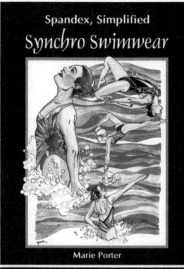

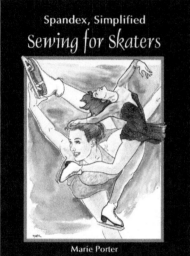

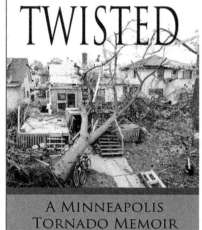

Introducing the "Spandex Simplified" Series

Prior to her cake career, Marie Porter had an illustrious career in spandex costuming. Now, you can learn all of her secrets to spandex design and sewing!

"Synchro Swimwear", "Sewing for Skaters" and "Sewing for Gymnasts" are the first three titles in Marie's new Spandex Simplified series, and are all about designing and creating spectacular and durable competitive sports costuming.

These books are appropriate for beginner to advanced levels of sewing ability, and is written from both a designer, and former "performance" athlete's point of view. They teach everything from the basics, to tricks of the trade. The "Spandex Simplified" series will prepare the reader to design and make almost any design of competitive synchro suit, skating dress, or gymnastics leotard imaginable.

Given the cost of decent competition suits, these manuals each pay for themselves with the savings from just one project!

The books are written completely in laymans' terms and carefully explained, step by step. Only basic sewing knowledge and talent is required. Learn everything from measuring, to easily creating ornate applique designs, to embellishing the finished suit in one book!

For a complete table of contents listings, current releases, and more info,

visit www.spandexsimplified.com

Twisted: A Minneapolis Tornado Memoir

On the afternoon of May 22, 2011, North Minneapolis was devastated by a tornado. Twisted recounts the Porters' first 11 months, post tornado. Rebuilding their house, working around the challenges presented by inadequate insurance coverage. Frustration at repeated bouts of incompetence and greed from their city officials. Dealing with issues such as loss of control, logistics, change, and over-stimulation, as two adults with Aspergers.

With the help of social media – and the incredibly generous support of the geek community – the Porters were able to emerge from the recovery marathon without too much of a hit to their sanity levels. New friends were made, new skills learned, and a "new" house emerged from the destruction. Twisted is a roller coaster of emotion, personal observations, rants, humor, social commentary, set backs and triumphs. Oh, and details on how to cook jambalaya for almost 300 people, in the parking lot of a funeral home… should you ever find yourself in the position to do so!

For wholesale inquiries or to purchase directly, visit

www.celebrationgeneration.com

CPSIA information can be obtained
at www.ICGtesting.com
Printed in the USA
LVOW05s2259250216

476754LV00017B/107/P